I0434870

FINAL
Bitter Lake National Wildlife Refuge
Comprehensive Conservation Plan

Roswell, New Mexico

Prepared for:

United States Fish and Wildlife Service
Region 2
500 Gold S.W.
Albuquerque, New Mexico 87103

Prepared by:

Research Management Consultants, Inc.
1746 Cole Blvd. Suite 300
Golden, Colorado 80401

September 25, 1998

COMPREHENSIVE CONSERVATION PLAN APPROVAL
for the
Bitter Lake NWR, Roswell, NM
1998

The attached Comprehensive Conservation Plan for the Bitter Lakes NWR was prepared for the Service by Research Management Consultants, Inc. (RMCI), Golden, Colorado, under the supervision of Regional and Refuge staff. The contents and format are found to be in compliance with Service policy on the preparation of Comprehensive Conservation Plans, and is hereby submitted for approval.

Submitted by:

9-20-98

Thomas P. Baca, M.P.A., Senior Natural
Resource Planner

Date

Approved by:

9-22-98

Bill Radke, Refuge Manager
Bitter Lake NWR

Date

Concurrence by:

9/24/98

Renne Lohoefener, Geographic ARD

Date

Concurrence by:

9/28/98

Nancy Kaufman
Regional Director, Region 2
U.S. Fish and Wildlife Service

Date

Table of Contents

Appendices

VISION

Bitter Lake National Wildlife Refuge (NWR) contains the most biologically significant wetlands in the Pecos watershed within New Mexico. This unique unit of the National Wildlife Refuge System plays a crucial role in the conservation of wetlands in the desert southwest, and protects a huge number of species, some endemic to the area, which inhabit these aquatic systems. Much of the habitat used by these species is associated with springs, sinkholes, and lakes fed from the Roswell groundwater basin. Additionally, the refuge straddles the Pecos River and is important for migratory birds and native river fishes. During the past decade many research efforts have focused on the unique set of species associated with the aquatic resources of the refuge. Yet much remains to be learned at Bitter Lake NWR, and management of the biological resources protected by the refuge have implications for rivers and springs throughout the southwest. The area is dominated by complex resource management issues. A diversity of human cultures continues to compete for limited access to water rights. Activities associated with agriculture, oil and gas development, mining, and urbanization have placed increasing demands on the landscape and identified the need for more responsible utilization of land and water resources that support the remaining native ecosystem components.

While providing for human opportunities to reasonably enjoy the magnificence of its rare resources, Bitter Lake NWR must continue to provide protected habitat for the diverse array of native plants and animals that rely upon the aquatic resources of the refuge for survival. The foreseeable future is one of protection and enhancement of the existing landscape, and active research and management for a diversity of native species at every trophic level within both upland and wetland environments on the refuge. With continually improving data gathering and analysis, better decisions can be made regarding natural resource conservation, leading to the secure abundance and population recovery of rare and/or state and federally listed endangered species such as the Pecos puzzle sunflower, Roswell spring snail, Pecos pupfish, barking frog, Western ribbon snake, interior least tern, and least shrew.

The Service envisions cooperative working relationships with other federal and state agencies along with non-governmental organizations and the interested public to accomplish its complex mission. These progressive working relationships will result in the refuge's improving role in protecting resources from negative impacts while still providing a wide range of wildlife-dependent opportunities and activities. Bitter Lake NWR continues to contribute to economic development and enhancement of the quality of human life in the middle Pecos River Valley. As local communities become more and more aware of this, the refuge will increasingly be promoted as a regional tourist destination. Such attention must be channeled to focus on the mission and benefit of the National Wildlife Refuge System, and the promotion of an increased understanding and support for the U.S. Fish and Wildlife Service efforts to protect native fish and wildlife and their habitats.

Executive Summary

The Comprehensive Conservation Plan (CCP) for the Bitter Lake NWR will serve as a management tool to be used by the Refuge staff and its partner's in the preservation and restoration of the ecosystem's natural resources. In that regard, the plan will guide management decisions over the next five to ten years and set forth strategies for achieving Refuge goals and objectives within that time frame.

The results of the planning process are perhaps best summarized by six major Refuge goals that are supported by a series of objectives and specific implementation strategies. Those goals include:

GOAL I: To restore, enhance and protect the natural diversity on the Bitter Lake NWR including threatened and endangered species by: (1) appropriate management of habitat and wildlife resources on refuge lands; and (2) by strengthening existing, and establishing new cooperative efforts with public and private stakeholders and partners.

GOAL II: To restore and maintain selected portions of a hydrological system that more closely mimics the natural processes along the reach of the Pecos River adjacent to the Bitter Lake NWR by: (1) restoration of the river channel, as well as restoration of threatened, endangered and special concern species; and (2) control of exotic species and manage trust responsibilities for maintenance of plant and animal communities and to satisfy traditional recreational demands.

GOAL III. "To offer compatible wildlife-dependent public access and recreational opportunities to include compatible forms of hunting, wildlife observation and photography, and continue wildlife interpretation and educational efforts."

GOAL IV. To protect and maintain cultural resources on the Bitter Lake NWR for the benefit of present and future generations.

GOAL V. To strengthen interagency and jurisdictional relationships in order to coordinate efforts with respect to refuge and surrounding area issues, resulting in decisions benefiting fish and wildlife resources, while at the same time avoiding duplication of effort.

Goal VI. To effect improvements to staffing and funding that will result in long-term enhancement of habitat and wildlife resources in the area of ecological concern, and allow the achievement of the goals of this plan and the goals of the National Wildlife Refuge System.

This document outlines objectives and strategies designed to effect the achievement of the goals enumerated above. The strategies include but are not necessarily limited to the following:

- A restoration of 250 acres of Research Natural Areas and 1000 acres in other areas by removal and control of non-native salt cedar;

- Restoration of over story vegetation near the refuge headquarters (10 acres) and providing appropriate irrigation;
- Restoration of 140 acres of abandoned agricultural fields as grasslands;
- Enhance promotion of environmental education in area schools and organizations on the value of short grass prairie ecosystems;
- Acquire identified land parcels as appropriate as they become available on a willing seller basis;
- Restoration of 100 acres of habitat associated with 25 gypsum sinkholes;
- Conversion of non-productive farmlands to seasonal wetlands / moist soil units;
- Construction and upgrade of all-weather road for wildlife tour route.

1.0 INTRODUCTION AND REGIONAL SETTING

The Bitter Lake National Wildlife Refuge (NWR) consists of 24,536 acres in three units located along the Pecos River, northwest of Roswell, Chaves County, New Mexico. The North Tract occupies approximately 12,160 acres and encompasses the 9,620 acre, Salt Creek Wilderness. The Middle Tract is comprised of approximately 11,000 acres and contains the refuge headquarters, Bitter Lake, several sinkholes and natural wetlands, desert uplands, riparian areas, agricultural croplands and impoundments. The South Tract consists of approximately 1,400 acres of primarily agricultural crop land and is closed to all public access.

Bitter Lake NWR was established on October 8, 1937 by Executive Order 7724 "as a refuge and breeding ground for migratory birds and other wildlife." Additional laws direct station activities. These include the Migratory Bird Conservation Act (16 U.S.C. 715d), which identifies the refuge "for use as an inviolate sanctuary, or for any other management purpose, for migratory birds." The Refuge Recreation Act (16 U.S.C. 460-1) identifies the refuge as being "suitable for incidental fish and wildlife-oriented recreational development, the protection of natural resources, and the conservation of endangered species or threatened species." The Wilderness Act of 1964 (P.L. 88-577) directs the Service to "maintain wilderness as a naturally functioning ecosystem" on portions of the refuge.

While originally established to save wetlands vital to the perpetuation of migratory birds, the isolated gypsum springs, seeps, and associated wetlands protected by the refuge have been recognized as providing the last known habitats in the world for several unique species. Bitter Lake NWR provides habitat for at least 352 bird species, 57 mammal species, 52 reptile and amphibian species, and 24 fish species. Management emphasis on the refuge is placed on the protection and enhancement of habitat for endangered species and federal candidate species, maintenance and improvement of wintering crane and waterfowl habitat, and monitoring and maintenance of natural ecosystem values. Habitat management to maintain populations of important neotropical migrants, shorebirds, and resident species associated with the lower Pecos ecosystem are also major objectives. Large numbers of migratory birds utilize the refuge, supported by refuge wetlands on the Middle Tract, and irrigated cropland on the South Tract.

1.1 Refuge and Ecosystem Challenges

Challenges

- Maintenance and restoration of Refuge buildings.
- Road Maintenance
- Production and efficient distribution of visitors brochures
- Improving community outreach
- Oil and gas exploration and encroachment on the Refuge
- Grazing and cattle trespass

- Implementation of appropriate wilderness management for the Salt Creek Wilderness
- Exotic species removal

Potential

- Increasing and utilizing moist soils for waterfowl food production
- Revegetation of native species
- Increased interpretive information on the auto loop tour
- Land acquisition to improve management efforts and reduce encroachment by development
- Pecos River channel restoration

2.0 PLANNING PERSPECTIVES AND CONSIDERATIONS

2.1 National Wildlife Refuge System

The Service is the principal agency responsible for conserving, protecting, and enhancing fish and wildlife and their habitats. The Service manages a diverse network of more than 500 National Wildlife Refuges, a system which encompasses 92 million acres of lands and waters. National Wildlife Refuges are established for specific purposes and provide habitat for thousands of species of birds, mammals, fish, and insects. Other refuges within the southern New Mexico area include the San Andres NWR located approximately 140 miles to the southwest near Las Cruces, New Mexico and the Bosque Del Apache NWR located approximately 140 miles to the northwest near Soccorro, New Mexico.

2.2 The Service & Ecosystem Management

While this plan focuses primarily on Service lands within the Area of Ecological Concern[1], there is a larger defined area following the Rio Grande and Pecos drainage systems. The Service has defined 52 ecosystems within the United States based primarily upon watershed designations. The Middle Rio Grande Watershed and the Pecos Watershed are considered biomes endemic to the desert and riparian areas of both river systems.

Based upon a broad set of issues present throughout the entire defined Ecosystem, the Service has developed some broad goals. These Ecosystem goals include:

GOAL I: To maintain and restore native terrestrial habitats along the Pecos River drainage.

GOAL II: To restore and maintain a hydrological system that mimics the natural processes along the Pecos River drainage.

2.3 Refuge Management Tracts

Bitter Lake NWR is comprised of the following three property tracts:

- The Upper or Northern Tract which consists of approximately 12,160 acres and encompasses the 9,620 acre, Salt Creek Wilderness, as well as the two acre Inkpot Research Natural Area (RNA).

- The Middle Tract which is comprised of approximately 11,000 acres and contains the refuge headquarters, Bitter Lake, several sinkholes and natural wetlands, desert

---

[1] An "Area of Ecological Concern" can be defined as: An essentially complete ecosystem (or set of interrelated ecosystems) of which one part can not be discussed without considering the remainder" [Malheur National Wildlife Refuge Master Plan and environmental Assessment, 1985. pg 7] The area of ecological concern referred to in this document is the Roswell Basin.

uplands, riparian areas, agricultural croplands and impoundments. This area also includes the Lake St. Francis and Bitter Lake (RNAs).

- The South Tract consists of approximately 1,400 acres of primarily agricultural cropland and is closed to all public access.

2.4   Planning Perspectives

This comprehensive management planning effort will integrate four perspectives so that the management direction over the next 10-15 years will produce comprehensive management approaches for the refuge lands and to the degree cooperative ventures permit, the Pecos River Ecosystem and Roswell Basin Area of Ecological Concern.

The three management planning perspectives are as follows:

1.   A natural resource conservation and protection perspective for the Pecos River Ecosystem relates the Service's commitment to protecting and restoring biome and ecosystem functions, structure, and species composition;

2.   A more narrow yet regional perspective for Roswell Basin Area of Ecological Concern issues; (i.e., contaminants, revegetation, endangered species and biological diversity, non-native species management, recreational use, water and air quality, inter-jurisdictional cooperation, socioeconomic considerations, etc.); and

3.   A focused perspective for the Refuge's habitat and wildlife management activities, cooperative efforts with partners, wilderness protection, compatibility of other uses, water rights, research and monitoring, archeological and historical resources, and improving public appreciation of refuge resources.

An understanding of these three perspectives and the relationship between them leads to the formulation of an integral set of refuge goals, objectives, and management actions/strategies for the next 10 to 20 years.

2.5   The Issues

The following is a list of the general issues that confront the Bitter Lake NWR programs. Goals and objectives have been designed to effect habitat restoration and protection of existing habitat for the benefit of a diversity of wildlife including endangered species.

10

Issue 1. Maintenance and restoration of native terrestrial habitats along the Pecos River drainage.

- Habitat Management
- Fire Management
- Cattle trespass

The selective use of fire and water management, as well as the removal of non-indigenous exotic species such as salt cedar, and the preservation and reintroduction of native species would be required to restore the native terrestrial habitats along the Pecos River drainage.

Fire Management is an essential natural tool to the maintenance and restoration of natural habitats within the Pecos River Ecosystem. Continued prescribed burning and fire manipulation will be an essential part of the overall habitat restoration strategy. The Bitter Lake NWR draft Fire Management Plan addresses these strategies, and the issues associated with them.

Management of some exotic species on the Refuge must be dealt with to protect the integrity of ecosystem values, provide natural balance within existing food webs, and to prevent unnatural conditions from altering the environment to the degradation of native plants and animals. Exotics, including carp, feral pigs, starlings, house sparrows, rock doves, salt cedar, kochia, knapweed, Russian thistle, and other species have been identified on the Refuge as having a detrimental effect on ecosystem values. These species will be removed from the Refuge whenever the opportunity presents itself. Control of such species will be evaluated and conducted on a case by case basis using the appropriate management tool. Natural revegetation by indigenous plants such as alkali sacaton and baccharis (seep willow) will be allowed to take place spontaneously. Selected pole plantings will be considered only in areas supported by favorable water and alkalinity conditions.

Cattle trespass from surrounding lands onto the Refuge can upset efforts to restore natural conditions and vegetation. Efforts to reduce the incidence of Cattle trespass include adequate fence construction and maintenance, and coordination with adjacent landowners.

Each of these activities would require careful planning and involvement with public and private stakeholders.

Issue 2. Maintenance and restoration of a hydrological system that mimics to the extent possible the natural processes along the Pecos River drainage within the Refuge.

- Water Resources, Water Rights, and Water Monitoring
- Channel Restoration
- Endangered Fish Recovery

Water Resources, Water Rights, and Water Monitoring:

Water resource management is a central component of the wildlife management effort at Bitter Lake NWR. The central theme of the water management strategy is to mimic the natural hydrological processes along the Pecos River drainage. Additionally, there are crucial water monitoring obligations that must be met by the Service. Educating the public about this process while offering compatible wildlife-dependent public access and recreational opportunities will always pose a challenge.

Pecos River Channel Restoration:

Much of the refuge lies within the historic flood plain of the Pecos River, and prior to upstream dam construction, flood flows would periodically change the river course within the flood plain. Various fish species adapted to this type of dynamic river channel, and some species became absolutely dependent upon this type of system. The Pecos bluntnose shiner is a federally listed threatened species with critical habitat that has declined drastically due to post dam conditions of the river. Some of the best potential habitat for this species occurs on Bitter Lake NWR. Downstream reaches of the river are extremely incised and channelized, providing little more than an "irrigation canal" which rapidly sweeps larval fish into Brantley Reservoir where habitat conditions are unfavorable and predatory fish are abundant.

Portions of the Pecos River channel on the refuge were also channelized in the past, speeding up water flow and removing the natural diversity within the river channel by isolating portions of the old river channel from the free-flowing Pecos. A proposed project would reconnect hydrologically isolated oxbows on the refuge to the existing river in an effort to provide more natural habitats for native fish and other wildlife including waterfowl, neotropical birds, and resident reptiles, amphibians, and mammals.

River channel restoration would require surveying river elevations, using bulldozers and excavators to reconnect oxbows to the flowing river, removing exotic salt cedar which has invaded and negatively impacted portions of these oxbows, and monitoring hydrologic and biotic changes. The project has intense support from other Service divisions, various state and federal agencies including both the Bureau of Reclamation and the Army Corps of Engineers, and local non-government organizations. The Bureau of Reclamation has already obligated funds to initiate planning for the project.

A Scope of Service for the proposed Pecos River Channel Restoration within the refuge was prepared by the Bureau of Reclamation during 1997, with intensive follow-up planning completed by FLO Engineering, Inc. consultants based in Breckenridge, CO. If completed as proposed, this project will result in localized conditions which are as close as possible to pre-dam conditions of the Pecos River. The Service believes that the higher degree of instability which occurred naturally along this reach of the river can be restored through reconnecting selected oxbows which are currently isolated from the mainstream Pecos River and through identifying changes that could be made to the existing river channel to restore habitat. However, caution must be used to prevent creating conditions in which the Pecos has an opportunity to damage existing facilities such as dikes, irrigation wells, and managed seasonal and permanent wetlands. An adaptive management approach will be cost effective and allow an evolution of the best strategies for meeting restoration objectives. It is our hope that one of the goals of this project is for the river to begin re-creating, and ultimately maintain, the complexity and dynamics required to promote native fish and wildlife diversity consistent with recovery plans to benefit federally listed species such as the Pecos bluntnose shiner.

Pecos River Channel Restoration Issues:

Budget and funding sources.
Protection of existing facilities (well, moist soil fields, dikes, roads)
Protection of existing biological values which are currently isolated from the river.
Potential bank erosion remedies along Hunter Oxbow.
Impacts to current refuge users (hunters, birders).
Contaminant issues from maintaining flow through longer stretch of the refuge.
Potential impacts to the Hwy. 380 bridge due to upstream channel instability.
Compliance/Permitting issues.
Small scale channel improvements to encourage channel instability.
Monitor biological values of currently isolated oxbows.

Endangered Fish Recovery:

The ultimate goal of threatened or endangered fish recovery on the refuge is to improve the status of such species to the point that survival is secured and the fish can be down listed or delisted. Maintenance and enhancement of existing fish populations and habitats is being accomplished on the refuge through population monitoring and enhancement of habitat through the removal of exotic salt cedar from Bitter Creek, Sago Spring, and ultimately all sinkholes with priority to those which contain the endangered Pecos gambusia. Reestablishment of fish within portions of their historic range is being accomplished on the refuge by surveying every sinkhole on the refuge and documenting salinity, conductivity, temperature, and dissolved oxygen content. Fish could then be transplanted into appropriate sites. Lastly, the Service needs to disseminate information to the public about threatened and endangered fish to gain support for protection. This is currently being accomplished at Bitter Lake NWR through the development and installation of two separate interpretive signs which discuss the importance of native fish management at Bitter Lake NWR.

Issue 3. Public Use and Environmental Education

- Improving Public Use and Environmental Education
- Management of the Salt Creek Wilderness

The public use and environmental education goal at Bitter Lake NWR is to strengthen existing interpretative programs and develop new approaches toward developing and disseminating information on the ecological importance of all forms of plants and animals protected by the refuge, and how biological diversity contributes to an increasingly healthy environment for all life, including humans. The refuge offers compatible wildlife dependent public access on most areas within the Bitter Lake NWR boundary through the provision of wildlife observation, photography, environmental education, and hunting where such uses are determined to be legally compatible with the purposes of the refuge. In a 1994 compatibility determination, fishing was found to be incompatible with the management of Bitter lake NWR.

Refuge headquarters provides a visitor reception area, which offers brochures, interpretive panels, and a large aquarium stocked with representable native fish protected on the refuge. Four indoor panels will be mounted at refuge headquarters by the autumn of 1998, and will include: "A Community of Plants and Animals, "Protecting Native Fish," "Rest Stop for Birds," and "Salt Creek Wilderness." At headquarters, visitors have an opportunity to meet Service employees and receive answers to any questions they might have. Public restrooms are also available at headquarters, which is typically open weekdays from 7:30 AM - 4 PM. The refuge provides staff to assist with field trips which are arranged in advance for students or other groups. Refuge staff also serve as guest presenters in classrooms or other settings.

Bitter Lake NWR is identified as a Watchable Wildlife site in New Mexico, and the most popular public use activity on the refuge is wildlife observation. Traditionally, late fall and early winter are the most popular times for visitors who come to witness the large and noisy concentrations of ducks, geese, and sandhill cranes. Two formally designated watchable wildlife sites are located on the refuge at the Middle Tract's Unit-5 overlook and at the South Tract along State Highway 380. These overlooks include wheelchair accessible, raised wooden platforms, which will be completed with interpretive signs by the autumn of 1998. The three outdoor panels scheduled to be mounted at the Unit-5 overlook will include: "A Community of Plants and Animals", "Working for Wildlife", and "Protecting Native Fish". The three outdoor panels scheduled to be mounted at the South Tract overlook will include: "A Community of Plants and Animals", "Working for Wildlife", and "J.P. White, Jr., Man with a Vision".

An 8-1/2-mile auto tour route circles most refuge wetlands and provides visitors an opportunity to view a variety of habitats and diverse wildlife. Unfortunately, this route is currently only a rough, dirt roadway, and is closed during wet weather due to muddy conditions. Visitors have had to have their vehicles towed out of the mud, leaving poor impressions of government service and limiting use by many who view the tour route with anxiety. A Refuge Operational Needs (RONS) project totaling $250,000 has been proposed to have base course gravel hauled, deposited, and graded onto the surface of the existing dirt roadway to improve driving conditions, eliminate dust, and allow safe all-weather use of the public tour route.

A variety of wildlife oriented activities attract visitors to the refuge. Photography is popular with both amateurs and professionals with typically about 20% of visitors indicating on visitor registers that they were taking photographs during their visit. Bicycling has become more popular and is limited only to the established tour route. Horseback riding is limited to the 10,000-acre North Tract, and is the most popular activity in the Salt Creek Wilderness.

Camping is allowed on the Salt Creek Wilderness by Special Use Permit only, but few visitors make use of this rugged area for backpacking or camping due to the lack of drinking water in the area. The refuge also provides a small camping area about one mile east of headquarters for organized scout and youth groups. The area is available to groups between October and April each year by Special Use Permit only.

Management of the Salt Creek Wilderness

Current management of the Salt Creek Wilderness follows the Bitter Lake NWR Salt Creek Wilderness Management Plan. This plan was completed in 1981 and relies on using the minimal tool, equipment, or structure necessary to accomplish the management objectives.

Within the Salt Creek wilderness, existing and potential easements, rights of way, and access issues must be dealt with which may potentially conflict with traditional wilderness management. The challenge will be to implement consistent and appropriate solutions to these issues while abiding by the goals of the Salt Creek Wilderness. Basically, existing legitimate right holders will be provided reasonable access to their operations or facilities which are located within the wilderness area. However, such right holders must provide the refuge manager a proposed plan of operation, describing methods and other aspects of the job with sufficient advance notice to allow service review of the proposal. The refuge manager will review the proposal and prescribe potential stipulations, mitigation, or alterations to the proposal to provide reasonable access while protecting trust resources and wilderness values. Authorized access will typically be required to remain on existing routes.

Broad goals of the Salt Creek Wilderness include:

1) To provide for the long term protection and preservation of the area's wilderness character under a principle of non-degradation. The area's natural condition, opportunities for solitude, opportunities for primitive and unconfined types of recreation, and any ecological, geological, or other features of scientific, educational, scenic, or historical value present will be managed so that they will remain unimpaired.

2) To manage the wilderness area for the use and enjoyment of visitors in a manner that will leave the area unimpaired for future use and enjoyment as wilderness. The wilderness resource will be dominant in all management decisions where choice must be made between preservation of wilderness character and visitor use.

3) To manage the area using the minimal tool, equipment, or structure necessary to successfully, safely, and economically accomplish the objective. The chosen tool, equipment, or structure should

be the one that least degrades wilderness values temporarily or permanently. Management will seek to preserve spontaneity of use and as much freedom from regulation as possible.

4) To manage non-conforming but accepted uses permitted by the Wilderness Act and subsequent laws in a manner that will prevent unnecessary or undue degradation of the area's wilderness character. Non-conforming uses are the exception rather than the rule; therefore, emphasis is placed on maintaining wilderness character.

The management plan set forth in this document reaffirms these goals.

Issue 4. Archaeological and Cultural Resources Preservation:

- Archaeological Resources
- National Natural Landmark
- Research Natural Areas

While numerous extensive archaeological sites are known to exist on Bitter Lake NWR, these sites have not been well documented or examined. These cultural resources need to be assessed and an appropriate action plan developed for their protection.

Management of the Bitter Lake Group National Natural Landmark and the Bitter Lake, Inkpots and Lake St. Francis Research Natural Areas (RNA) is incorporated into the general goals for the refuge. The major issues regarding these areas are the same issues that confront the Refuge as a whole such as habitat management and restoration and encroachment of the refuge by gas exploration drilling and land development.

Issue 5. Strengthening interagency and jurisdictional relationships to resolve surrounding area issues.

- Gas Exploration and Development adjacent to the Refuge Middle Tract
- Encroaching development
- Coordination of efforts and eliminating duplication of effort.

Increasing cooperation with other agencies and jurisdictions would help alleviate many of the surrounding area issues The Service has had several meetings with Bureau of Land Management (BLM) since 1993 concerning the issue of developing extensive natural gas leases in the Pecos River flood plain just off the north boundary of the refuge Middle Tract. The Service has consistently recommend that this proposal requires an Environmental Impact Statement because the cumulative impacts to the environment are immense.

The Service's greatest remaining concerns continue to relate to potential impacts on the ecosystem through possible contamination of groundwater and the potential negative alteration of the aquifer and its associated springs, seeps, and sinkholes occurring on the refuge adjacent to the proposed action. The Pecos River and the refuge's springs and sinkholes provide essential habitat for numerous aquatic special status species including the Pecos bluntnose shiner, Pecos gambusia, Pecos pupfish, Koster's tryonia, Roswell springsnail, and Pecos assiminea. While some of these essential habitats on the refuge are outside the 100-year floodplain, all are influenced by the "artesian aquifer" through which the proposed action will be drilling into. It seems clear that potential negative impacts to aquatic habitats may occur from surface disturbing activities and from well drilling into the substrate. Environmental contamination is one possible result, as is alteration of groundwater gradients which supply springs and seeps on the refuge. The potential impacts to threatened and endangered species, which are otherwise protected within Bitter Lake NWR, is significant.

Several questions need to be answered before any proposed drilling should proceed. For example, information should be collected on the gradients of groundwater associated with the proposed project within each distinct aquifer. Information should also be collected on the connectivity of the aquifers to help determine their conduits. The sources of water in each of the biologically crucial springs and sinkholes located on the refuge should be determined. If methods for determining answers to these questions could be developed, ultimately a groundwater model of the region including the refuge could be constructed to synthesize the above information for use as a tool for determining potential contamination and water mixing scenarios. Development of such a model might be the ultimate mitigation required of the applicant for oil and gas exploration and development adjacent to sensitive environments.

The Service is also concerned about the cumulative impacts of any proposed well drilling activities, and believes that any stepped approach of evaluating incremental actions could be used to inadequately evaluate the potential impacts of the entire proposed action. Significant cumulative impacts can result from individually minor but collectively significant actions taking place over a period of time. An environmental impact statement could accurately address the entire proposed action of well drilling for oil and/or natural gas in proximity to the refuge, and would accurately assess incremental impacts associated with the entire project. Working closely with other agencies to produce such a document is a reasonable approach to assess alternatives and avoid significant adverse impacts.

Working more closely with other agencies and jurisdictions would also offer a reasonable approach to solving the encroachment of land development adjacent to the Refuge. Such close relationships could also be used to reduce duplication of effort and to share resources.

Issue 6. Acquisition of sufficient staffing and funding to accomplish Refuge goals.

Acquiring the needed staffing and funding increases to accomplish the Refuge goals will be essential to completion of the goals.

2.6   The Need for Action

The Service's Refuge Manual states that the purpose of comprehensive management planning is to "provide long range guidance for the management of national wildlife refuges." [4 RM 1.1, Planning] Planning provides a road map to facilitate the kind of coordination that is necessary to enhance the efficiency of implementing management actions designed to benefit the Bitter Lake NWR, and the Area of Ecological Concern. The Service's approach will be to offer management goals, objectives, strategies/management actions that are consistent with ecologically desirable outcomes for the entire Pecos River Ecosystem.

2.7   Expected Planning Outcomes

The following outcomes were designed to be consistent with the Service Manual's comprehensive management planning objectives. The planning effort should bring about the following outcomes:

1. The planning effort will ensure that legal mandates and national direction are incorporated in the management of the Bitter Lake NWR;

2. The planning effort should determine the capability of the Refuge to further the Service and the Refuge System goals, objectives, and long-range plans and to provide a means of evaluating accomplishments;

3. The planning effort should provide a systematic process for making and documenting refuge decisions;

4. The planning effort should establish broad management strategies that are to the degree possible, consistent with the ecosystem perspective for the area, and should guide the refuge management programs and activities consistent with an ecosystem perspective;

5. The planning effort should provide continuity in the management of the Refuge;

6. The planning effort should provide a practical basis for budgeting requests to implement management programs leading to the achievement of refuge objectives; and,

7. The planning effort should achieve an optimum level of public acceptance and/or support for the management strategies adopted through effective involvement in the planning process.

2.8   Public Involvement

In an ongoing effort to involve the local community and officials in the CCP process, the Service and RMCI prepared and distributed a fact sheet in August 1997. The fact sheet describes the CCP process and defined the comment period. The fact sheet was mailed in early August 1997 and the 45-day comment period started August 25, 1997 and ended October 8, 1997. An information repository has also been established and is maintained with information relevant to the refuge for public review. The repository is located at the Roswell Public Library in Roswell, New Mexico. RMCI continues to update the mailing list based on response from interested parties. Public meetings may be provided if necessary, based on public response to the CCP process. A draft CCP and Environmental Assessment (EA) were released July 1, 1998. The Service published a formal notice in the Federal Register requesting comments and advice from the public.[2] Comments were received, considered, and to the degree possible, they have been incorporated into this document.

---

[2] Federal Register, Vol 63, No. 126, p 35939, Notice of Intent to Issue 2 Draft Comprehensive Conservation Plans and Associated Environmental Assessments for 2 National Wildlife Refuges in the Southwest Region. This notice pertained to the release of the San Andres NWR and Bitter Lake NWR CCP/ EA draft documents.

3.0   RESOURCE DESCRIPTION

Pecos River Ecosystem Definition

The Pecos River is the largest tributary sub-basin of the Rio Grande originating in the Sangre De Cristo Mountains of North Central New Mexico. The Pecos River is confluent with the Rio Grande at what is now Amistad Reservoir near Laredo, Texas. Hydrologically, the Pecos River represents a hybrid of Rocky Mountain and Plains stream systems, containing equally important snow melt and summer rain components of the annual hydrograph. At its origin the River drains crystalline rocks of the Southern Rocky Mountains with high water quality. Below Fort Sumner, New Mexico, the River enters a naturally saline basin comprised primarily of evaporitic sedimentary rocks, resulting in higher salinity loads. This area is famous for its karst topography and artesian spring systems.

The area supports plant and animal communities adapted to the diverse and unique habitats within the region. Anthropogenic modifications to the habitats have caused range reductions and in some cases extirpation of native plants and animals. For example, the introduction of a non-native plant commonly called salt cedar. Salt cedar was used for bank stabilization in the 1940's and has significantly altered both the stream channel habitats and the native riparian plant communities. Construction and operation of dams for consumptive uses has further altered habitats and impacted native aquatic communities.

The area has complex resource management issues. Diverse human cultures competing for water rights (dating to 1800's) and growing resource demands have led to the depletion and contamination of ground and surface water. Impacts from previous water and land management practices for agricultural needs have seriously altered the Pecos Ecosystem, reducing native species habitats and diversity. Other associated impacts include oil and gas development, mining, and urbanization.

The proposed management priorities for the Pecos River Ecosystem focus on trust resources, including traditional roles (recreation oriented) and more recent directions regarding biodiversity and conservation issues. This plan addresses aquatic and terrestrial components separately and each in concert with riparian issues.

Area of Ecological Concern General Make-up

The Bitter Lake NWR lies within the Roswell Basin of southeastern New Mexico. The Roswell Basin is a natural hydrologic basin that extends from the summits of the Capitan, Sacramento, and Guadalupe Mountains on the west to just beyond the Pecos River on the east. Bitter Lake NWR lies near the eastern edge of the basin along the west bank of the Pecos River. Groundwater flow in the basin is from west to east. Bitter Lake NWR lies in the discharge zone for the basin, with ground water flowing from the artesian zone to springs which maintain the wetlands and surface water impoundments of the Refuge. Because any impacts to the aquifer of the Roswell Basin could impact the water quality at the discharge points at Bitter Lake NWR, the Roswell Basin is considered the "Area of Ecological Concern".

3.1   Vegetation

Vegetation on the refuge consists primarily of mixed Chihuahuan shrub/grassland with areas of riparian vegetation. The South Tract is a working farm and as a result is dominated by cultivated plants. The shrub vegetation is dominated by four wing saltbush (Atriplex) and is associated with a scattering of mesquite, creosote and iodine bush. The grassy understory is dominated by alkali sacaton, salt grass, and gyp grama. Areas adjacent to the water courses contain riparian vegetation composed primarily of coyote willow, seepwillow, and exotic salt cedar. Cottonwoods occur only in scattered patches influenced by freshwater springs.

3.2   Wildlife

To date 352 bird species have been documented on the refuge, including 44 nesting species. In addition 57 mammal species, 40 reptile species, 12 amphibian species, and 24 fish species have been identified on the refuge and surrounding area.

A variety of wetlands exist on Bitter Lake NWR, ranging from relatively fresh water flowing streams, to brackish impoundments and natural sinkholes, to hypersaline playa lakes. Each of these wetland types has an intricate community of aquatic invertebrates and associated vegetation and native fish. While the diversity of fish has been well documented, baseline inventories of aquatic invertebrates are almost unknown. Extremely superficial sampling by individuals over the past 15 years has revealed three new snail species and one new amphipod species which were not previously known to science. The potential for discovery of numerous new endemic species is great due to the unique geology, isolation, and diversity of habitats. Aquatic invertebrates provide a prey base for many vertebrate species and are an important part of the natural food web. It is uncertain to what extent these invertebrates play in the stability of ecosystems. Additionally, it is important to discern the distribution of endemic life forms on the refuge and identify unique areas which need greater attention and protection. Sampling, analysis, and identification of species is crucial to understanding the basis of the ecosystem protected by the refuge.

The refuge typically winters over 20,000 snow geese, Ross' geese, and Canada geese, and up to 10,000 lesser sandhill cranes. Marshbird, waterbird, and shorebird populations reach over 2,500 each spring and fall. While originally established to save wetlands vital to the perpetuation of migratory birds, the isolated gypsum springs, seeps, and associated wetlands protected by the refuge have been recognized as providing the last known habitats in the world for several unique species. These include Koster's springsnail, Roswell springsnail, and Noel's amphipod. Additionally the refuge contains some of the best protected habitats in New Mexico for the Pecos puzzle sunflower, Pecos assiminea snail, Mexican tetra, Pecos pupfish, Pecos Gambusia, greenthroat darter, arid land ribbon snake, interior least tern, and least shrew. Each of these species is listed by the federal government and/or state of New Mexico as threatened or endangered.

Bitter Lake NWR provides a critical role in maintaining a sanctuary for at least 28 special status species (federal and/or state listed) and has often been referred to as the endangered species refuge in the state.

3.3 Climate

Annual rainfall in the Roswell area averages 12.25 inches per year with an average of 7.4 inches of snow. Temperatures typically range annually from near 0°F in winter to 110°F in summer with average lows of 41.2°F in January and average highs of 83.7°F in July. The wet season usually runs from mid-June to late August and the average relative humidity is 48%.

Table 1. Temperature and Rainfall Data Collected at Bitter Lake NWR During 1997.

Month	Avg. High	Avg. Low	Range	Precipitation
January	44°F	20°F	81 to 8 °F	0.90"
February	--	24	-- to 16	1.96
March	--	31	-- to 19	--
April	72	40	88 to 26	3.06
May	81	51	95 to 41	1.13
June	88	57	101 to 44	1.86
July	97	63	103 to 55	1.05
August	94	62	101 to 55	1.26
September	89	56	100 to 47	2.02
October	75	41	95 to 22	1.30
November	64	27	85 to 16	0.95
December	50	25	68 to -9	2.49
		TOTAL MOISTURE		17.98"*

*Minimum; no precipitation data was collected for 20 days in March.
This data represents typical annual rain fall and temperature at Bitter Lake NWR.

3.4 Geology

Bitter Lake NWR is located in the Lower Pecos Valley Subsection of the Great Plains Physiographic Province of Southeastern New Mexico. Much of the Pecos Valley Section is underlain by Permian bedrock units composed of gypsiferous and saline evaporites, limestone and dolomite, mudstone, shales, and sandstone. Dissolution of evaporite and carbonate units is an active geomorphic process affecting landscape evolution in much of the region, and various sizes of solution-subsidence depressions are common landforms. From essentially the headwaters of the Pecos River, the sedimentary rocks of limestones, shales, and sandstones dip off the mountains in an easterly direction to form a large continuous regional aquifer system. The permeability of the aquifers varies considerably depending on the degree of dissolution or fracturing that has taken place. These processes have been most active in the southern part of the area and have resulted in the well known Roswell Artesian Basin. The limestone aquifer south of Roswell is the ancient Capitan reef in which the Carlsbad Caverns were formed by percolating groundwater.

3.5   Soils

Soils in the area are dominated by aridisols, which are not well suited for dryland agriculture because they lack the necessary moisture to support any long term growth except arid-adapted vegetation. The soil horizon is low in organic matter and is light in color. Aridisols also exhibit special fertility problems due to unavailable micronutrients resulting from a high pH.

3.6   Water Management

Refuge wetlands are vital to the perpetuation of migratory birds. In addition, the isolated gypsum springs, seeps, and associated wetlands protected by the refuge have been recognized as providing the last known habitats in the world for several unique species. Water manipulation is crucial to managing optimum diversity and abundance of fish and wildlife on the refuge. While full-to-the-brim lake levels may be attractive to human visitors, such levels are not a natural situation, and static water levels are truly death to an aquatic system.

The refuge has about 1,200 surface acres of water in the form of natural lakes, impoundments, sinkholes, and streams. Yet this entire area is subject to over six feet of evaporation annually. While the water easily evaporates due to high temperatures and constant winds, the salts and other solids in the water do not evaporate, rather, they have concentrated over the years. The practice of attempting to maintain all pond and lake levels on the refuge at their maximum capacity has resulted in waters which are extremely salty, in some cases much saltier than seawater. Salt water holds significantly less dissolved oxygen, which is crucial to all fish and aquatic insects upon which fish and many birds feed.

Since 1994, to help control salinity and manage refuge waters for all of the fish and wildlife which utilize the refuge, lake levels have been manipulated (sometimes drastically) to flush accumulated salts. Many of the lakes are left low during hot summer months when evaporation is highest. Exposing mud flats during spring, summer, and early fall provides feeding areas for abundant shorebirds which absolutely require these shallow areas to forage in. The salt flats exposed during spring and summer also provide an important nesting area for snowy plovers, avocets, and least terns which otherwise would concentrate their nests along lake edges where they are much more susceptible to predators. Some lakes are kept low during winter months to provide shallow roosting areas for sandhill cranes and snow geese.

Water management on the refuge essentially mimics the natural dropping and rising of wetland water levels in accordance with natural processes. For the most part, refuge lakes are filled to capacity during the fall and winter to provide roosting and feeding areas for migratory waterfowl. Wetlands

23

are slowly flooded to continually inundate vegetation grown during the summer which makes a steady supply of food available for migratory birds as they arrive. These same wetlands are slowly lowered during the spring to provide feeding areas for migratory shorebirds and other waterbirds.

Bitter Lake National Wildlife Refuge sits at a juncture between the Roswell Artesian Groundwater Basin (Roswell Basin) and the Pecos River (Pecos). These two systems and their interactions account for the diversity of water resources on the Refuge including sinkholes, springs, wetlands, oxbow lakes, and riverine habitats. Protecting levels within the Roswell Basin and the nature and timing of flows in the Pecos are important components of species conservation on and surrounding the Refuge. The Refuge's federally reserved water rights essentially protects ground water levels of the Roswell Basin in the Refuge vicinity. Actions associated with the conservation of the federally threatened Pecos bluntnose shiner hold promise for the maintenance of minimal flows on the Pecos.

The Roswell Basin historically maintained groundwater levels that were 80 feet above the Refuge's mean topographic surface (mts, 3500 feet). This level dropped to 20 feet above mts in the 1970's and since then has been on the rise towards the current level of 40 feet above mts. The Roswell Basin supplies water for the sinkholes, springs and seeps of the Refuge. A higher groundwater level translates to increased habitat. The Refuge has recently undergone the adjudication of their federally reserved water rights by the State of New Mexico (order signed May 1997). These rights essentially protect ground water levels on and near the Refuge from declining below the modern conditions as defined by monthly average conditions within the period 9/1996 through 9/2000 barring drought conditions. Ground water trends within the Roswell Basin suggest that spring flows will continue to increase and sinkhole levels will continue to rise in the near future.

The nature and timing of flows within the Pecos River have been significantly altered by reservoir operations. Prior to the 1937 installation of Sumner Reservoir in Fort Sumner New Mexico; 1) base flows of the Pecos through the Refuge rarely dropped below 80 cfs, where today they drop below 30 cfs roughly 50% of the time and 10 cfs 20% of the time, 2) the ten year flood recurrence was 10,000 cfs where today it is 2000 cfs. Roswell Basin inflows guarantee perennial flows from just north of the Refuge to Brantley Reservoir. A minimal flow of 35 cfs just north of the Refuge (at the Acme gauge) is a recommendation of the 8 year Pecos River Investigation for the bluntnose shiner (which translates to a minimal flow of roughly 40 cfs at the Refuge). Due to flood control constraints, increasing maximum discharge out of Sumner Reservoir is currently not being considered. Such flows are very important for both in stream and riparian habitat since they hydrologically connect the main channel with the floodplain and allow for local sediment storage. Future conservation efforts associated with water on the Refuge should focus on the Pecos River since this is where the least assurance of biologically sound hydrology exists.

In support of ongoing water right claims, a comprehensive water measurement system requires ongoing monitoring to gather important information toward justifying water needs on the refuge. This entire system of equipment is composed of two surface water measuring stations, five shallow piezometers, a multilogging water quality/climate station, and a series of staff gauges installed at every impoundment and at Bitter Lake, Hunter Marsh, and South Weir. In addition to gathering information from the various gauges and equipment on a periodic basis, a network of surface water points need to be measured monthly to help determine the relationship between surface water and ground water on the refuge. Salinity and conductivity are monitored at various locations throughout the year to help relate water quantity with water quality.

In a legal "Stipulation Concerning the Reserved Water Rights of the United States for Bitter Lake National Wildlife Refuge," the Service claimed rights for the amount of water necessary to maintain open water surface acreage in the Middle Unit of the refuge as follows:

January	-	1100 acres
February	-	800 acres
March	-	900 acres
April	-	500 acres
May, June, July	-	400 acres
August	-	600 acres
September	-	1100 acres
October	-	1200 acres
November, December	-	1100 acres

An important issue became the accuracy of what exactly our minimum water needs are to biologically support the mission of the refuge[3]. While the Service used the best information it had available to liberally determine impoundment surface acre needs on a monthly basis, the legal stipulation requires these figures be refined to best meet fish and wildlife objectives. It was determined that a five year monitoring requirement as part of the stipulation would allow the Service to formally refine our water needs, and would accurately document our realistic federal reserved surface water right determinations.

If any of the five year monthly averages determined for these impoundments is equal to or greater than the amount claimed for that month in the stipulation, the amount of the reserved surface water right for open water surface acreage for that month will be the amount claimed. If any of the five year monthly averages is determined to be lower than the amount claimed for that month, then the amount of the reserved right for that month will be the amount of the five year monthly average. The reserved water right ultimately depends on what is a "normal" year. If it is determined that the five years of monitoring represent an unusually dry period, then, at the option of the United States, additional years of data will be collected until a period of five consecutive years that is not unusually dry is achieved. Five years of monitoring is considered to be an unusually dry period if during any one year: the five year moving average of monthly water levels at the United States Geological Survey's Berrendo Recorder Well falls below 3535 feet mean sea level, or the five year moving

---

[3] Crucial to this stipulation is a legal agreement to monitor the surface acreage and volumes of impounded wetlands for the months of March, June, August, and October for five years (September 1996 through September 2001) and determine for those months the maximum surface acreage and volume for each of the following eight impoundments: Bitter Lake (Unit-4), Unit-3, Unit-5, Unit-6, Unit-7, Unit-15, Unit-16, and Hunter Marsh. This will essentially require Service personnel to monitor water gauges set in place at each impoundment on a monthly basis and then use an established table to determine the surface areas and volumes of each impoundment.

average of monthly stream flow gains in the Pecos River between the USGS's Acme and Artesia stream gaging stations falls below 17 cubic feet per second.

The stipulation also set forth conditions associated with the United States' claims to reserved surface water rights for surface flow in Bitter Creek and its associated seeps and springs, essentially a right to in-stream flow. These claims in Bitter Creek as measured at the Bitter Creek Flume are as follows[4]:

January	- .6 cfs	July	- .15 cfs
February	- .6 cfs	August	- .2 cfs
March	- .45 cfs	September	- .25 cfs
April	- .25 cfs	October	- .3 cfs
May	- .2 cfs	November	- .5 cfs
June	- .15 cfs	December	- .6 cfs

Using this data, five year monthly averages will be derived by averaging the monthly mean flows of the five measurement years. Again, if the flow is equal to or greater than the amount claimed for that month, the amount of reserved surface water right for surface flow in Bitter Creek for that month will be the amount claimed. If any of the five year monthly averages are determined to be lower than the amount claimed, the water right for Bitter Creek for that month will be the amount of the five year monthly average. The same drought conditions pertinent to surface acres of impoundments explained above also apply to Bitter Creek surface water rights[5].

State personnel can also monitor the flows in Bitter Creek and the surface acreage and volume of refuge impoundments, but must notify the Refuge Manager prior to entering the refuge to make measurements and obtain prior approval from the Refuge Manager before entering any closed areas of the refuge.

3.7   Fire Management

Effective fire management is not only important for the protection of human life and property, but it is also an essential tool for habitat maintenance and restoration. The importance and complexity of fire management is reflected in the decisions, findings and objectives of the draft Fire Management Plan for the Pecos Fire Management Complex which includes Bitter Lake NWR.

Significant decisions and findings contained within the draft plan are as follows:

---

[4] The Service will monitor the flow at the Bitter Creek Flume for five years (September 1996 through September 2001) and determine the daily mean flows which will be averaged to determine the monthly mean flows. A water recorder is already in place which continuously monitors flow in Bitter Creek, requiring occasional visits to download data.

[5] The Service is obligated to provide our data regarding impoundment surface acreage and volume to the State Engineers Office on a yearly basis, and to provide our data regarding surface flows in Bitter Creek to the State Engineers Office on a quarterly basis.

- Fires have occurred frequently within the complex and have the potential to exceed several thousand acres in size. Fires can best be described as fast moving, low intensity surface fires.

- Lightning caused fires are a routine natural phenomena within the southern plains and have had a major ecological influence in the maintenance of some shrub-free grasslands within the complex.

- Two Fire Suppression Units have been established within the complex: 1) The CONFINE/CONTAIN suppression strategies will be used in the Minimum Impact Unit which dominates the interior portion of the refuge and contains a wide variety of sensitive flora/fauna, 2) the more aggressive CONTROL strategy will be employed within the Mutual Threat Unit around the exterior of the refuge (within the urban interface) and on Hatchery Lands.

- The construction of a fuel break network is required in order to effectively implement the Fire Management Plan. While existing physical barriers will be utilized whenever possible, some additional fuel breaks will require construction/maintenance within both the refuge and the hatchery. As proposed, some of the fuel breaks within the refuge will occur in designated wilderness and must be specifically approved as the minimum tool necessary for the administration of the area.

- Prescribed fire will be used throughout the complex to reduce hazardous fuels and to accomplish specific resource management objectives (especially salt cedar control and wildlife habitat improvement). An estimated 5,000 acres per year will be treated, conclusive for prescribed burn programs at both the hatchery and refuge.

- The complex will host an aggressive and comprehensive fire management program with participation required at all levels within the USFWS. Non-fire funded field station employees will be encouraged to become involved and several staff positions have been identified as critical to the long term implementation of the program.

- Interagency communications and cooperation is essential for the full and effective implementation of this plan. The complex will maintain cooperative agreements with local, state and federal departments for assistance in fire suppression and prescribed burning.

Fire management program objectives for the complex are listed as follows:

- Protect human life and property both within and adjacent to the refuge, through the implementation of a comprehensive fire management program.

- Suppress all wildfire in an efficient, cost effective manner, while minimizing environmental impacts from unwarranted suppression activities.

- Mitigate (rehabilitate) human induced impacts to resources or natural processes.

- Reduce hazardous fuels accumulations and the potential for wildfire in areas surrounding station development and values (facilities) at risk.

- To the degree practical, utilize management ignited prescribed fire to maintain, mimic and/or restore natural ecosystem processes and native plant and animal communities. More specifically, to create favorable habitat conditions required by all forms of native wildlife, especially resident fish populations and migratory birds and listed species that in part depend on the sanctuary of the refuge and hatchery for their survival.

- Monitor and evaluate the effects of fire management on refuge ecosystems.

- Facilitate scientific investigation and research in order to refine burning prescriptions and program objectives.

- Promote an interagency approach to managing fire and fire based ecosystems through the development of cooperative agreements and use of the Incident Command System.

- Actively participate in wild-land fire mobilizations through cooperation with national, regional, and management zone authorities.

- Provide a spectrum of interpretive and educational programs designed to foster understanding, recognition, and acceptance of the refuge fire management program.

- Conduct a fire prevention program in cooperation with other agencies.

- To manage all station fire activities in accordance with the above program objectives.

In 1996 Bitter Lake NWR became the fire management coordinator for all National Wildlife Refuges and National Fish Hatcheries (11 stations) in New Mexico and West Texas. These additional responsibilities require that Bitter Lake NWR provide support and expertise to the broader area. This requires that Bitter Lake NWR have the required personnel, equipment, and funding needed to accomplish these objectives.

3.8   Cultural and Historic Resources Features

While numerous extensive archaeological sites are known to exist on Bitter Lake NWR, these sites have not been well documented or examined. Bits of black on white pottery, brown earthware, stone arrowheads, metates, fire rings, worked fish scales, and other artifacts have been observed in several upland areas on the refuge. While these sites currently appear to be relatively secure from vandalism and looting, some of the sites are in close proximity to well used public use areas and require immediate evaluation and protection. Baseline analysis must be conducted so that any detrimental changes can be documented over time. Either a Service archaeologist or contract archaeologists could conduct this work with some refuge staff assistance

The Lake St. Francis sinkhole cluster and Bitter Lake proper on the Middle Tract (Appendix I, Exhibit 1), plus the Salt Creek Wilderness on the Northern Tract (Appendix I, Exhibit 2) have been designated as the Bitter Lake Group, a Registered National Natural Landmark. The Bitter Lake Group was included in the National Registry of Natural Landmarks on August 11, 1980, under the authority of the Historic Sites Act of 1935. The area encompasses approximately 10,090 acres.

Bitter Lake Group National Natural Landmark:

The National Natural Landmarks Program was established by the Secretary of the Interior in 1962, under authority of the Historic Sites Act of 1935 (16 U.S.C. 461 et seq) to identify and encourage the preservation of the full range of geological and ecological features that are determined to represent nationally significant examples of the nation's natural heritage. Sites for possible National Natural Landmark designation are evaluated by the National Park Service, and, if determined nationally significant, are recommended to the Secretary of the Interior for designation. Once a landmark is designated, it is included on the National Registry of Natural Landmarks, which currently lists about 600 National Natural Landmarks nationwide, including 12 in New Mexico. Federal agencies are required to consider the unique properties of these nationally significant areas under the National Environmental Policy Act, and the Secretary of Interior is required to provide an annual report to the Congress on damaged or threatened National Natural Landmarks.

The 10,090-acre Bitter Lake Group National Natural Landmark was designated on the refuge in August 1980. The areas comprising this group contain sinkhole depressions formed by solution of gypsum-bearing rocks resulting in caverns and collapsed domed roofs. Most contain highly saline artesian water. The landmark supports shrub-grassland vegetation representative of the northern Chihuahuan Desert, with alkaline resistant species on lake shores and bottomlands. The group has three major qualifying features. Salt Creek Wilderness Area offers an excellent example of an ecological community significantly illustrating the process of succession and restoration to natural conditions following disruptive change. This area also supports an isolated remnant marine algae (*Bataphora oerstedii*) in the Inkpot sinkhole. The inland occurrence of this algae is unique, and represents a relic flora persisting from an earlier period. Other than Bitter Lake NWR, this marine algae is found only in lagoons along the Gulf of Mexico. Lake St. Francis Natural Area contains examples of a habitat supporting a vanishing, rare, or restricted species, the Pecos gambusia and the Pecos pupfish. A secondary qualifying feature is the presence of over 30 natural sinkholes in the Lake St. Francis Natural Area which offer a major refugium for the two fish species.

The biggest immediate threats to the Bitter Lake Group National Natural Landmark and to aquatic refuge resources are proposals to drill for natural gas adjacent to the north boundary of the refuge Middle Tract and to begin production of an existing gas well within the Salt Creek Wilderness. The proposed action is significant because of its proximity to the refuge, its proximity to the National Natural Landmark, its proximity to Lake St. Francis Research Natural Area and Bitter Lake Research

Natural Area, and its potential adverse impacts to aquifers, spring flows, and other habitats critical to threatened and endangered species.

Bitter Lake Research Natural Area

A Research Natural Area is a land-management category used by federal agencies since 1927 to designate lands permanently reserved for research and educational purposes. Natural processes are supposed to dominate in these tracts, which preserve some natural feature or features. Principal goals in protecting these lands are: 1) to preserve a representative array of all significant natural ecosystems as sources of baseline data, against which the effects of human activities in similar environments can be measured, 2) to provide sites for studies of natural processes in undisturbed ecosystems, and 3) to provide gene pool preserves for plant and animal species, especially rare ones. Agencies have developed similar regulations to achieve protection of scientific and educational values in research natural areas. The guiding principle is to prevent unnatural encroachments. All kinds of human manipulation are discouraged, and public uses that might impair natural values are generally discouraged. Scientists who wish to use a Research Natural Area on refuge land must obtain a Special Use Permit.

New Mexico has 17 Research Natural Areas, three of which are located on Bitter Lake NWR. The 300-acre Bitter Lake RNA is located a mile north-northwest of refuge headquarters, and is dominated by the Bitter Lake playa. In winter, large numbers of waterfowl, sandhill cranes, and migratory shorebirds inhabit the lake, and species such as the snowy plover nest here. The depth of Bitter Lake ranges from 0-4 feet, and receives water from Bitter Creek, Lost River, Dragonfly Spring, and Sago Spring on its west side. These aquatic systems, along with several associated sinkholes, provide unique habitat for three uncommon native fish species: the Pecos gambusia, greenthroat darter, and Pecos pupfish. Koster's spring snail, Roswell spring snail, Pecos assiminea, and Noel's amphipod are four invertebrates which represent relict species once associated with Permian shallow seas which covered the area. Some of these species are now found only on the refuge and in a privately owned sulphate-rich spring on the nearby Roswell Country Club. The playa basin is thought to be the result of subsidence caused by an underground stream. Water levels depend on flow in the Roswell Artesian Basin, which in turn depends upon precipitation and water use many miles to the west and south. The principal threat to the natural area is the fall of watertables in the Roswell Artesian Basin. Some of the small sinkholes in the west part of the RNA have become dry and water flow from the springs and creeks has decreased over the years.

Lake St. Francis Research Natural Area

The 700-acre Lake St. Francis Research Natural Area is located two miles north-northwest of refuge headquarters and encompasses about 30 small, round, steep-sided sinkholes. These sinks formed by collapse of overlying strata into hollows formed by solution of pockets of gypsum. All sinks at one time held water, and several still do. The largest sinkhole is Lake St. Francis, which is 200-feet across and 60-feet deep. Water level varies from one sink to another, but all are alike in that levels have declined since the 1950's. Variations in water level apparently depend on the artesian water level, which in turn depends on ground water recharge rates in the Hondo and adjacent basins to the west, mostly in Lincoln County.

Quality of the brackish water varies, but several sinkholes support unique native fish and invertebrate communities. Bitter Creek, a small intermittent stream, flows southward through the west side of the RNA into Bitter Lake. Streamflow into Bitter Creek is augmented by Dragonfly Spring, Lost River, and Sago Spring. Some of the sinkholes, including Lake St. Francis, contain the marine green algae *Bataphora oerstedii* of which the known distribution includes only coastal waters and lagoons from Bermuda to the Gulf of Mexico, plus these sinkholes. The occurrence of this algae, along with three mollusk species, identify the significance of this area as a relict habitat for species more common during the Permian Periods when shallow seas covered this part of New Mexico. During 1937, the major sinkholes were connected by ditches to divert excess flow to man-made impoundments east of Bitter Lake. Water levels in the sinkholes have declined well below ditch levels which have not flowed since the 1950's. While the area has been invaded by salt cedar and Russian olive, the principal threat to this RNA is the problem of drying springs and ponds and increased salinity of the ground water that supplies the surviving springs. The watertable in the recorder well six miles southwest of Lake St. Francis declined 25 feet between 1959-1977, and water use in the basin continues to increase.

Inkpot Research Natural Area

The two-acre Inkpot RNA is located within the Salt Creek Wilderness on the North Unit of the refuge. The chief feature is the "Inkpot," a vertical-walled sinkhole 150-feet in diameter and 90-feet deep. The Inkpot is located at the edge of the scenic Red Bluffs, a 50-foot Permian escarpment which runs across the north end of the refuge. In 1937, this sinkhole was overflowing and feeding a second, lower sink, which was also full and overflowed through a half-mile stream to a playa lake in the Salt Creek valley floor west of the Pecos River. Water levels in Inkpot have steadily declined and are presently about 18-feet below the spill point. Like the other sinkholes in the area, Inkpot formed when artesian water dissolved gypsum deposits causing overlying strata to collapse. Surface runoff enlarged the sink until it connected with channels leading from the artesian aquifer, allowing artesian water to rise in the sink. Inkpot contains the marine algae *Bataphora oerstedii* and a population of endangered Pecos gambusia. Falling water tables, due in part to increased use of water in the Roswell Artesian Basin, and perhaps partly due to declining precipitation, are the greatest threat to Inkpot RNA.

Salt Creek Wilderness

The 9,621-acre Salt Creek Wilderness was established under PL-91-504 on October 23, 1970. The Wilderness Act defines wilderness as an area of undeveloped federal land retaining its primeval character and influence, without permanent improvements or human habitation, which is protected and managed so as to preserve its natural conditions.

The topography of the area is generally rolling, but is frequently cut by small arroyos and drainages. The northern quarter of the tract contains a line of red clay-gypsum bluffs, towering up to 75-feet above the lowlands. Scattered throughout the northern half of the tract lie at least 21 gypsum sinkholes. Formed by the dissolving of underlying strata and subsequent collapse of the surface dome, these sinks vary in surface diameter from 60 to 200 feet and are from less than 20 feet to over 100 feet deep. Most of the shallow sinks are now dry due to the general lowering of the water table in the area. The deeper sinks, however, still contain water and some are connected with an artesian system and hold water year-round. At one time the Inkpot sinkhole flowed enough surplus water to maintain a shallow 60-acre lake at the northeast corner of the Wilderness.

During the late 1800's and into the early 1900's this area was significantly overgrazed and otherwise impacted by cattle ranching. During the early 1900's, at least three homesteads were established on the area, and limited farming began along with continued grazing. In 1937, the Service purchased the land, which at that time still contained ample marshland associated with artesian springs and Salt Creek, a perennial stream. Permitted grazing use of the tract finally ceased in 1955, refuge farming to provide food for waterfowl ceased during the 1960's, and the area was evaluated as a Wilderness Study Area in 1968. With designation as a wilderness in 1970, all permanent refuge structures were demolished and removed, existing ground water rights were transferred to the middle unit of the refuge, and the Service began to manage the Wilderness as a "naturally functioning ecosystem." Scientific research, vegetation management, wildlife management, and monitoring programs all in accordance with the Service's minimum tool policy are crucial to meet this broad goal. The area currently provides opportunities for primitive recreation, including hiking, equestrian use, hunting, and sightseeing. Three "developments" still exist within the Salt Creek Wilderness. An underground natural gas pipeline, installed along a right-of-way in the early 1950's, crosses the tract diagonally from northeast to southwest, a distribution power line extends along much of the south Wilderness boundary, and an active natural gas well lease occurs in the southwest corner of the area. These developments should be withdrawn by the Service as opportunities become available.

3.9   Socio-economic Features

Bitter Lake NWR is located approximately nine miles from the city of Roswell, New Mexico, with a population of approximately 50,000. Several other small towns are within thirty to ninety miles away. The predominant land uses in the vicinity of the refuge are grazing and irrigated farming. There is some oil and gas well activity in the area.

The Roswell Chamber of Commerce lists the refuge as one of the area's main attractions. The refuge has been averaging about 38,000 visitors per year. The majority of visitors are from nearby locations and it is estimated that ten to twenty percent of the visitors are from distant locations. Visitation was dramatically higher in 1996 with a total of 52,713 visitors. The increase reflects attempts by the refuge staff to promote awareness of the refuge locally and may represent a trend towards increased visitation. Additionally, New Mexico State Highway and Transportation Department is currently planning significant highway improvements in the Roswell area which suggest increased growth and visitation to the Roswell area.

The refuges annual budget is approximately $600,000 dollars and the majority of this money is recycled in the local economy due to refuge staff living within the Roswell area and the utilization of the local stores. Additionally the Youth Conservation Corp (YCC) hires several youths, many of them local for summer work.

3.10   Refuge Staffing

In order to accomplish Refuge goals, Full staffing will be required (Appendix K). Current staffing at Bitter Lake NWR consists of the following positions:

1.   Project Leader GS-0486-13 Permanent Full Time (PFT)
2.   Refuge Operations Specialist GS-0485-7/9/11 PFT
3 .   Fire Management Officer GS-0401-12 PFT
4.   Wildlife Biologist GS-0486-7/9/11 PFT
5.   Office Assistant GS-0303-06 PFT
6.   Biological Technician GS-0404-07 PFT
7.   Maintenance Worker WG-4749-08 PFT
8.   Maintenance Worker WG-4749-05 PFT
9.   Prescribed Fire Specialist GS-0401-7/9 PFT
10.   Range Technician (Engine Boss) GS-0455-06 PFT
11.   Range Technician GS-0455-05 Term Full Time (TFT)
12.   Range Technician GS-0455-05 TFT
13.   Youth Conservation Core (YCC) Group Leader GS-0186-05 TFT

4.0 LEGAL, POLICY, AND ADMINISTRATIVE GUIDELINES, AND OTHER SPECIAL CONSIDERATIONS

This Section outlines current legal, administrative, and policy guidelines for the management of national wildlife refuges. It begins with the more general considerations such as laws and executive orders for the Service, and moves toward those guidelines that apply specifically to the Bitter Lake NWR.

This unit also includes sections dealing with specially designated sites such as historical landmarks and archaeological sites, all of which carry with them specific direction by law and/or policy. In addition, consideration is given to guidance prompted by other formal and informal natural resource planning and research efforts.

All the legal, administrative, policy, and planning guidelines provide the framework within which management activities are proposed and developed. This guidance also provides the framework for the enhancement of cooperation between the Bitter Lake NWR and other surrounding jurisdictions in the ecosystem, including BLM, BOR and Chaves County.

4.1 Legal Mandates

Administration of the refuges takes into account a myriad of bills passed by the United States Congress and signed into law by the President of the United States. These statutes are considered to be the law of the land as are executive orders promulgated by the President. The following is a list of most of the pertinent statutes establishing legal parameters and policy direction to the National Wildlife Refuge System. Included are those statutes and mandates pertaining to the management of the Bitter Lake NWR.

For those laws that provide special guidance and have strong implications relevant to the Service or Bitter Lake NWR, legal summaries are offered below. Many of the summaries have been taken from *The Evolution of National Wildlife Law* by Michael J. Bean.[6] For the bulk of applicable laws and other mandates, legal summaries are available upon request.

Summary of Congressional Acts, Treaties, and other Legal Acts that Relate to Administration of the National Wildlife Refuge System:

1. Lacey Act of 1900, as amended (16 U.S.C. 701).

2. Antiquities Act of 1906 (16 U.S.C. 431).

3. Migratory Bird Treaty Act of 1918 (16 U.S.C. 703-711) and 1978 (40 Stat. 755).

---

[6] Bean, Michael J., 1983. *The Evolution of National Wildlife Law*, Praeger Publishers, New York.

4. Migratory Bird Conservation Act, (1929) as amended. (16 U.S.C. 715-715s).

5. Migratory Bird Hunting Stamp Act of 1934, (U.S.C 718-718h).

6. Fish and Wildlife Coordination Act, (1934) as amended (16 U.S.C. 661-666).

> *The Act is "the first major federal wildlife statute to employ the strategy of compelling consideration of wildlife impacts. The act authorized 'investigations to determine the effects of domestic sewage, trade wastes, and other polluting substances on wildlife, encouraged the development of a program for the maintenance of an adequate supply of wildlife on the public domain' and other federally owned lands, and called for state and federal cooperation in developing a nationwide program of wildlife conservation and rehabilitation."[7]*

7. Historic Sites Act of 1935 (16 U.S.C. 461).

> *The Act declared it a national policy to preserve historic sites and objects of national significance, including those located on refuges. It provided procedures for designation, acquisition, administration, and protection of such sites. National Historic and Natural Landmarks are designated under authority of this Act. As of January 1989, 31 national wildlife refuges contained such sites.*

8. Convention Between the United States of America and the Mexican States for the Protection of Migratory Birds and Game Mammals, (1936) (50 Sta. 1311).

9. Convention of Nature Protection and Wildlife Preservation in the Western Hemisphere, 1940 (56 Stat. 1354).

10. Fish and Wildlife Act of 1956, as amended (16 U.S.C. 742-742j).

11. Refuge Recreation Act, as amended, (Public Law 87-714.76 Sta. 653; 16 U.S.C. 460k-4) September 28, 1962.

> *This Act authorizes the Secretary of the Interior "to administer areas of the System 'for public recreation when in his/her judgement public recreation can be an appropriate incidental or secondary use; provided, that such public recreation use shall be permitted only to the extent that it is practicable and not inconsistent with the primary objectives for which each particular area is established.' Recreational uses 'not directly related to the primary purposes and functions of the individual areas' of the System may also be permitted, but only upon an determination by the Secretary that they 'will not interfere with the primary purposes' of the refuges and that funds are available for their development, operation, and maintenance."[8]*

---

[7]   Ibid., pp. 181.

[8]   Ibid., pp. 125-126.

35

12. Refuge Revenue Sharing Act of 1964, (16 U.S.C. 715s) as amended (P.L. 95-469, approved 10-17-78).

> *The Act provides "that the net receipt from the 'sale or other disposition of animals, timber, hay, grass, or other products of the soil, minerals, shells, sand, or gravel, from other privileges, or from leases for public accommodations or facilities in connection with the operation and management'...of areas of the National Wildlife Refuge System shall be paid into a special fund. The monies from the fund are then to be used to make payments for public schools and roads to the counties in which refuges having such revenue producing activities are located."[9]*

13. Land and Water Conservation Fund Act of 1965, as amended (16 U.S.C. 460L-4 to 460L-11), and as amended through 1987.

14. National Wildlife Refuge System Administration Act of 1966 (16 U.S.C. 668dd-668ee).

> *This Act, derived from sections 4 and 5 of Public Law 89-669, "consolidated 'game ranges,' 'wildlife ranges,' 'wildlife management areas,' 'waterfowl production areas,' and 'wildlife refuges,' into a single 'National Wildlife Refuge System.' It (1) placed restrictions on the transfer, exchange, or other disposal of lands within the system; (2) clarified the Secretary's authority to accept donations of money to be used for land acquisition; and (3) most importantly, authorized the Secretary, under regulations, to 'permit the use of any area within the System for any purpose, including but not limited to hunting, fishing, public recreation and accommodations, and access whenever he determines that such uses are compatible with the major purposes for which such areas were established.'"[10]*

15. National Historic Preservation Act of 1966 (16 U.S.C. 470).

> *Public Law 89-665 as repeatedly amended, provided for preservation of significant historical features (buildings, objects, and sites) through a grant in aid program to the States. It established a National Register of Historic Places and a program of matching grants under the existing National Trust for Historic Preservation. As of January 1989, 91 historic sites on national wildlife refuges have been Placed on the National Register.*

16. National Environmental Policy Act of 1969, as amended (42 U.S.C. 4321-4347).

17. Protection and Enhancement of Environmental Quality Executive Order of 1970 (Executive Order 11514, dated March 5, 1970).

18. Environmental Education Act of 1975 (20 U.S.C. 1531-1536).

19. Use of Off-Road Vehicles on the Public Lands Executive Order of 1972, as amended (Executive Order 11644, dated February 8, 1972, as amended by Executive Order 11989, dated May 24, 1977).

---

[9] Ibid., pp. 126.

[10] Ibid., pp. 125.

20. Endangered Species Act of 1973 (16 U.S.C. 1531-1543 87 Stat. 884) P.L. 93-205). The Endangered Species Act as amended by Public Law 97-304, The Endangered Species Act Amendments of 1982, dated February 1983.

According to Bean, the 1973 Act "builds its program of protection on three fundamental units. These include two classifications of species--those that are 'endangered' and those that are 'threatened' -- and a third classification of geographic areas denominated 'critical habitats.'"[11]

The Act: (1) Authorizes the determination and listing of species as endangered and threatened, and the ranges in which such conditions exist; (2) Prohibits unauthorized taking, possession, sale, and transport of endangered species; (3) Provides authority to acquire land for the conservation of listed species, using land and water conservation funds; (4) Authorizes establishment of cooperative agreements and grants-in-aid to States that establish and maintain active and adequate programs for endangered and threatened wildlife; and, (5) Authorizes the assessment of civil and criminal penalties for violating the Act or regulations.

Section 7 of the Endangered Species Act requires Federal agencies to insure that any action authorized, funded, or carried out by them does not jeopardize the continued existence of listed species or modify their critical habitat.

21. Floodplain Management Executive Order of 1977 (Executive Order 11988, dated May 24, 1977). Wetlands Preservation Executive Order of 1977 (Executive Order 11988, dated May 24, 1977).

These executive orders require both the protection and the enhancement of wetlands and floodplain. Both were signed in May, 1977. When Federally owned wetlands or floodplain are proposed for lease or conveyance to non Federal public or private parties, both executive orders require that the agency: "(a) reference in the conveyance those uses that are restricted under Federal, State or local... regulations; and (b) attach other appropriate restrictions to the uses of such properties by the ... purchaser and any successor, ... or © withhold such properties from..." lease or disposal (E.O. 11990, 4, E.O. 11988, 3(d). In addition, each agency is required to "avoid undertaking or providing assistance" for activities located in wetlands unless (1) ..."there is no practicable alternative...", and (2)... "the proposed action includes all practicable measures to minimize harm...which may result from such use" (E.O. 11990, 2). The term "agency" is defined in both of these executive orders as having the same meaning as the term "Executive agency" which means an Executive department, a Government corporation, and an independent establishment.

22. The Archaeological Resource Protection Act of 1979 (P.L. 96-95, 93 Sta. 721, dated October 1979). (16 U.S.C. 470aa - 47011).

This Act largely supplanted the resource protection provisions of the Antiquities Act for archaeological items. It established detailed requirements for issuance of permits for any excavation or removal of archaeological resources from Federal or Indian Lands. It also established civil and criminal penalties for the unauthorized excavation, removal, or damage of any such resources; for any trafficking in such resources removed from Federal or Indian land in violation of any provision of Federal law; and for interstate and foreign commerce in such resources acquired, transported,

---

[11] Ibid., pp. 331.

or received in violation of any State or local law. Public Law 100-588, approved November 3, 1988, (102 Stat. 2983) lowered the threshold value of artifacts triggering the felony provision of the Act from $5,000 to $500, made attempting to commit an action prohibited by the Act a violation, and required the land managing agencies to establish public awareness programs regarding the value of archaeological resources to the Nation.

23. Fish and Wildlife Conservation Act of 1980 (P.L. 96-366, dated September 29, 1980). ("Nongame Act") (16 U.S.C. 2901-2911; 94 Stat. 1322).

> *Approved September of 1980, this Act authorized grants for development and implementation of comprehensive State nongame fish and wildlife plans and for administration of the Act. It also required the Service to study potential mechanisms for funding these activities and report to Congress by March, 1984. According to Bean, the Act "strives to encourage comprehensive conservation planning, encompassing both nongame and other wildlife...The impetus for the enactment of this legislation was the perception that animals not ordinarily valued for sport hunting or commercial purposes receive insufficient attention and funds from state wildlife management programs."*[12]

> *Public Law 100-653 (102 Stat. 3825), approved November 14, 1988, amended the Act to require the Service to monitor and assess nongame migratory birds, identify those likely to be candidates for endangered species listing, identify appropriate actions, and report to Congress one year from enactment. It also requires the Service to report at five year intervals on actions taken.*

24. Administrative Procedures Act (5 U.S.C. 551-559, 701-706, 1305, 3105, 3344, 4301, 5362, 7521; 60 Stat. 237), as amended (P.L. 79-404, as amended).

25. Bald Eagle Protection Act of 1940 (16 U.S.C. 668-668d; 54 Stat.), as amended.

26. Canadian United States Migratory Bird Treaty (Convention Between the United States and Great Britain (for Canada for the Protection of Migratory Birds. (39 Stat. 1702; TS 628), as amended.

27. Clean Air Act (42 U.S.C. 1857-1857f; 69 Stat. 322), as amended.

28. Convention on Wetlands of International Importance Especially as Waterfowl Habitats (I.L.M. 11:963-976, September 1972).

> *This Convention, commonly referred to as the Ramsar Convention, was adopted in Ramsar, Iran, February 3, 1971, and opened for signature at UNESCO headquarters, July 12, 1972. On December 21, 1975, the Convention entered into force after the required signatures of seven countries were obtained. The United Senate consented to ratification of the Convention on October 9, 1986, and the President signed instruments of ratification on November 10, 1986. The Convention maintains a list of wetlands of international importance and works to encourage the wise use of all wetlands in order to preserve the ecological characteristics from which wetland values derive. The Convention is self implementing with the U.S. Fish and Wildlife Service providing U.S. secretariat responsibilities and lead for Convention implementation.*

---

[12] Ibid., pp. 227.

29. Cooperative Research and Training Units Act (16 U.S.C. 753a-753b, 74 Stat. 733), as amended. P.L. 86-686).

30. Federal Aid in Fish Restoration Act (16 U.S.C. 777-777k, 64 Stat. 430).

31. Federal Aid in Wildlife Restoration Act (16 U.S.C. 669-669i; 50 Stat. 917), as amended.

32. Federal Environmental Pesticide Control Act of 1972 (7 U.S.C. 136-136y; 86 Stat. 975), as amended.

33. Federal Land Policy Management Act of 1976 (43 U.S.C. 1701-1771, and other U.S.C. sections; 90 Stat. 2743). Public Law 94-579, October 1976.

34. Federal Property and Administrative Services Act of 1949 (40 U.S.C. 471-535, and other U.S.C. sections; 63 Stat. 378), as amended.

35. Federal Water Pollution Control Act Amendments of 1972 (33 U.S.C. 1251-1265, 1281-1292, 1311-1328, 1341-1345, 1361-1376, and other U.S.C. titles; 86 Stat. 816), as amended.

36. Fish and Wildlife Improvement Act of 1978 (16 U.S.C. 7421; 92 Stat. 3110) P.L. 95-616, November 1978.

37. Flood Control Act of 1944 (16 U.S.C. 460d, 825s and various sections of title 33 and 43 U.S.C.; 58 Stat. 887), as amended and supplemented.

38. Freedom of Information Act (5 U.S.C. 552; 88 Stat. 1561).

39. Refuge Trespass Act (18 U.S.C. 41; Stat 686).

40. Transfer of Certain Real Property for Wildlife Conservation Purposes Act of May 1948, (16 U.S.C. 667b-667d; 62 Stat. 240), as amended.

41. Water Resources Planning Act (42 U.S.C., 1962-1962a-3; 79 Stat. 244), as amended.

42. Waterfowl Depredations Prevention Act (7 U.S.C. 442-445; 70Stat. 492), as amended.

43. Clean Water Act of 1972, Section 404.

> *Under this Act, permits are required to be obtained for discharges of dredged and fill materials into all waters, including wetlands. Implementation of the 404 program involves three other federal agencies in addition to limited state involvement. The Environmental Protection Agency (EPA), the National Marine Fisheries Service, and the Service review permit applications and provide comments and recommendations on whether permits should be issued by the Corps. EPA has veto authority over permits involving disposal sites if impacts are considered unacceptable. EPA also develops criteria for discharges and state assumption of the 404 program. Section 404 regulations were*

changed in 1984 due to a national lawsuit, and 404 jurisdictions now apply to tributaries of navigable waters and isolated wetlands and waters if interstate commerce is involved. With the new regulations, all washes, drainages, and tributaries of navigable waters, including ephemeral and perennial streams, are included under the 404 program in Texas.

44. The Food Security Act of 1985 (Farm Bill).

45. National Wildlife Refuge System Improvement Act of 1997 (H.R. 1420, 105th Congress).

   This law is the first "organic" act for the National Wildlife Refuge System. The Act amends portions of the National Wildlife Refuge System Administration Act and the Refuge Recreation Act, and reiterates into law Executive Order 12996.

4.2   Agency-Wide Policy Directions

Fish and Wildlife Service Agency Mission -- Since the early 1900s, the Service mission and purpose has evolved, while holding on to a fundamental national commitment to threatened wildlife ranging from the endangered bison to migratory birds of all types. The earliest national wildlife refuges and preserves are examples of this. Pelican Island, the first refuge, was established in 1903 for the protection of colonial nesting birds such as the snowy egret and the endangered brown pelican. The National Bison Range was instituted for the endangered bison in 1906. Malheur National Wildlife Refuge was established in Oregon in 1908 to benefit all migratory birds with emphasis on colonial nesting species on Malheur Lake. It was not until the 1930s that the focus of refuge programs began to shift toward protection of migratory waterfowl (i.e., ducks and geese). As a result of drought conditions in the 1930s, waterfowl populations became severely depleted. The special emphasis of the Service (then called the Bureau of Wildlife and Sport Fisheries) during the next several decades was on the restoration of critically depleted migratory waterfowl populations.

The passage of the Endangered Species Act of 1973 refocused the activities of the Service as well as other governmental agencies. This Act mandated the conservation of threatened and endangered species of fish, wildlife, and plants both through federal action and by encouraging the establishment of State programs. In the late 1970s, the Bureau of Wildlife and Sport Fisheries was renamed the U.S. Fish and Wildlife Service to broaden its scope of wildlife conservation responsibilities to include endangered species, as well as game and nongame species. A myriad of other conservation-oriented laws followed, including the Fish and Wildlife Conservation Act of 1980, which emphasized the conservation of nongame species.

The Service as a whole has no "organic" act to focus upon for the purposes of generating an agency mission. The agency mission has always been derived in consideration of the various laws (as listed in Section 2 of this Unit) and treaties that collectively outlined public policy concerning wildlife conservation. The Department of the Interior Manual states:

   "The U.S. Fish and Wildlife Service is responsible for conserving, enhancing, and protecting fish and wildlife and their habitats for the continuing benefit of people through Federal programs relating to

wild birds, endangered species, certain marine mammals, inland sport fisheries, and specific fishery and wildlife research activities.[13]

Refuge System: Mission and Goals

National Wildlife Refuge System: Mission and Goals

The National Wildlife Refuge System is the only existing system of federally owned lands managed chiefly for the conservation of wildlife. The system mission is a derivative of the Service mission. This mission was most recently revised in October 1997, by passage of the National Wildlife Refuge System Improvement Act (P.L. 105-57). This Act followed up on Executive Order 12996 (April 1996) Management of Public Uses on National Wildlife Refuges to reflect the importance of conserving natural resources for the benefit of present and future generations of people.

This Act amends the National Wildlife Refuge System Administration Act of 1966 in a manner that provides an "Organic Act" for the Refuge System. It will ensure that the Refuge System is effectively managed as a national system of lands, waters and interests for the protection and conservation of our nation's wildlife resources.

The Act gives guidance to the Secretary of the Interior in the overall management of the Refuge System. The Act's main components include a strong and singular conservation mission for the Refuge System, a requirement that the Secretary of the Interior maintain the biological integrity, diversity and environmental health of the Refuge System, a new process for determining compatible uses of refuges, and a requirement for preparing comprehensive conservation plans. The Act states first and foremost that the mission of the National Wildlife Refuge System be focused singularly on wildlife conservation.

The Refuge Improvement Act is an overarching Act with both general and specific elements that provide long term management direction for the Refuge System. It became law the day it was signed; however, pending development and approval of final rules and regulations, the Service has issued the following as interim policy guidance with respect to the Act's Sections:

Sec. 1 Purpose

> This Order provides guidance for implementing specific provisions of the National Wildlife Refuge System Improvement Act of 1997, pending development of new policies and regulations responsive to the Act.

---

[13] Departmental Manual 142 DM 1.1.

Sec. 2 <u>Scope</u>

This policy applies to management of the National Wildlife Refuge System.

Sec. 3 <u>Existing policy</u>

Existing policy and directives for management of the National Wildlife Refuge System remain in force except for those which are in conflict with provisions in the Act, in which case the Act prevails.

Sec. 4 <u>Mission of the National Wildlife Refuge System</u>

The mission of the National Wildlife Refuge System is:

"To administer a national network of lands and waters for the conservation, management, and where appropriate, restoration of the fish, wildlife, and plant resources and their habitats within the United States for the benefit of present and future generations of Americans."

Sec. 5 <u>Administration of the National Wildlife Refuge System</u>

a. The term "refuge" means a designated area of land, water, or an interest in land or water within the Refuge System, but does not include Coordination Areas.

b. Each refuge shall be managed to fulfill the mission of the Refuge System, as well as the specific purposes for which that refuge was established.

c. Each refuge shall be managed in a manner that maintains the biological integrity, diversity and environmental health of the Refuge System.

d. The status and trends of wildlife resources on each refuge shall be monitored.

e. The purposes of each refuge are the purposes specified in or derived from the law, proclamation, executive order, agreement, public land order, donation document, or administrative memorandum establishing, authorizing, or expanding a refuge, refuge unit, or refuge sub-unit.

f. Each refuge shall ensure effective coordination, interaction, and cooperation with neighboring landowners and appropriate state fish and wildlife agencies.

g. Each refuge shall cooperate and collaborate with other Federal agencies and appropriate state fish and wildlife agencies in refuge acquisition and management.

Sec. 6 Public Uses

a. When determined to be compatible, the following six wildlife-dependent recreational uses are the priority general public uses of the Refuge System: hunting, fishing, wildlife observation and photography, and environmental education and interpretation.

b. Compatible priority public uses shall receive enhanced consideration over other public uses in refuge planning and management.

c. Priority public uses are appropriate and legitimate uses of the Refuge System. Refuges are strongly encouraged to seek opportunities to permit these activities when ways can be found to ensure their compatibility. Reasonable efforts should be made to ensure that lack of funding is not an obstacle to permitting these uses through development of partnerships with the States, local communities and private and nonprofit groups.

d. The following general hierarchy between refuge activities and public uses will apply: Priority 1 - activities necessary to fulfill the refuge purposes and the Refuge System mission; Priority 2 - provide opportunities for wildlife-dependent recreational uses, when determined to be compatible. All other public uses will be a lower priority.

e. In providing priority public uses, refuges shall emphasize opportunities for families to experience compatible wildlife-dependent recreation, particularly opportunities for parents and their children to safely engage in traditional outdoor activities, such as fishing and hunting.

Sec. 7 Compatibility

a. Compatibility determinations prepared during the period between enactment of the National Wildlife Refuge System Improvement Act of 1997 (October 9, 1997) and issuance of a new compatibility policy will be made under the existing compatibility standards and process.

Sec. 8 Comprehensive Conservation Planning

The Act provides that Comprehensive Conservation Plans shall be completed for all refuge units within 15 years from the date of enactment.

4.3   Refuge Purpose Statements [14]

Formal establishment of a unit of the National Wildlife Refuge System is usually based upon a specific statute or executive order specifically enumerating the purpose of the particular unit. However, refuges can also be established by the Service under the authorization offered in such laws as the Endangered Species Act of 1973 or the Fish and Wildlife Act of 1956. In these cases, lands are identified by the Service that have the right elements to contribute to the recovery of a species or the maintenance of habitat types. Oftentimes, the Service works in cooperation with private nonprofit organizations in efforts to acquire suitable lands.

Bitter Lake NWR was established on October 8, 1937 by Executive Order 7724:

"…as a refuge and breeding ground for migratory birds and other wildlife."

The Migratory Bird Conservation Act (16 U.S.C. 715d), identifies the refuge:

"…for use as an inviolate sanctuary, or for any other management purpose, for migratory birds."

The Refuge Recreation Act (16 U.S.C. 460-1) identifies the refuge as being:

"…suitable for incidental fish and wildlife-oriented recreational development, the protection of natural resources, and the conservation of endangered species or threatened species."

---

[14]   Refuge purpose statements are primary to the management of each refuge within the refuge system. The purpose statement is the basis upon which primary management activities are determined. Additionally, these statements are the foundation from which "allowed" uses of refuge are determined through a defined "compatibility process."

The Wilderness Act of 1964 (P.L. 88-577) directs the Service to:

"...maintain wilderness as a naturally functioning ecosystem" on portions of the refuge.

5.0   BITTER LAKE NWR MANAGEMENT PROGRAM

The following goals, objectives, and strategies are, unless otherwise noted in the text, expected to be implemented throughout the five to ten year term of this plan. Due to the fact that the Bitter Lake NWR CCP is a working document, modifications to the following objectives and strategies are anticipated. Where applicable, the Refuge Operating Needs System (RONS) project number has been included with the associated strategy.

5.1   Biological Diversity, Land Protection, Wildlife and Habitat Protection

GOAL 1:   **To restore, enhance and protect the natural diversity on the Bitter Lake NWR including threatened and endangered species by: (1) appropriate management of habitat and wildlife resources on refuge lands; and (2) by strengthening existing, and establishing new cooperative efforts with public and private stakeholders.**

Objective 1:   Restore and maintain native grassland and riparian communities on 24,000 acres along the Pecos River an tributaries within the Refuge to meet the needs of native flora and fauna, and to secure a minimum amount of land acquisitions to sustain specific resource needs.

Strategies

1:    Strengthen existing and develop new cooperative efforts with federal and state agencies, and private landowners regarding interrelationships between wildlife, livestock, hydrology, public use and the ecosystem. Throughout the term of this plan the Refuge will provide technical assistance to public land owners on land management issues.

2:    Promote education in area schools and non-government organizations (NGO) on the value of the short-grass prairie ecosystem by conducting interpretive talks, providing four field days per year for school and NGO groups, upgrading the 8-mile auto tour route to include educational displays and brochures, and promoting research projects with area universities addressing problems wildlife and landowners face in the Pecos Valley.

3:    In cooperation with the appropriate agencies, develop and implement a fire program on selected federal lands that will achieve established objectives for flora and fauna communities. Use these programs as training, technical advice and ensuing support for area landowners.

4:    Develop a realistic revegetation policy in collaboration with federal and state agencies to restore the Pecos drainage with native vegetation (e.g., salt-cedar removal, willow, cottonwood, grass plantings). By 2001 develop a vegetation baseline map to allow for monitoring changes in uplands. Provide financial support, technical advice and incentives for land owners to revegetate with native willow, cottonwood, and grasses.

5: Restore approximately 1,500 acres of native vegetation along the Refuge reach of the Pecos River, and develop collaborative revegetation objectives for the Pecos drainage system as a whole.

6: Identify, prioritize and secure critical and unique habitat from destruction or further degradation through fee and easement acquisitions (Appendix I, Figure 6).

7: The Refuge will continue to manage the Salt Creek Wilderness in accordance with the existing wilderness goals reflected in this document. In accordance with the Wilderness Act of 1964, no vehicular access will be allowed. For access by mineral right (oil and gas) and leaseholders the manager is required to provide "reasonable" access. That access will be determined on a case-by-case basis. Prior to issuance of a permit to enter the wilderness for legitimate proposed development of oil, gas, or mineral rights, the manager will require from the owner of the rights a detailed plan to include the rationale necessary for the use of motorized or mechanized equipment, the scope and duration of development, and a mitigation plan in the event surface resources including access ways are disturbed.

8: Restore 250 acres in the Research Natural Areas and 1,000 acres in other sections of the Refuge by removal and control of exotic salt-cedar (RONS 96011, 94002, and 94005)by 2003.

9: Restore 10 acres of upland habitat near the Refuge headquarters by planting native overstory vegetation and providing appropriate irrigation (RONS 94003) by the year 2000.

10: Reseed 140 acres of abandoned fields that are too alkaline for crop production with native alkali sacaton and manage the area as native grasslands (RONS 94008) by 2005.

11: Restore 10 acres of Farming habitat through treatment to remove noxious johnson grass on the ten acres (RONS 94004) by 2001.

12: Preserve 65 acres of upland habitat through bank erosion control of the Pecos River (RONS 91010) by 2003.

Objective 2:   To successfully maintain and restore habitat for native wildlife including invertebrates, amphibians, reptiles, birds and mammals and provide wintering grounds for migratory birds (e.g., neotropical migrants, shorebirds and waterfowl). Approximately 1,000 acres of native habitat will be restored annually.

Strategies

1:    Monitor wildlife populations including neotropical migrants (e.g., passerine, shore and marsh birds, and waterfowl), reptile and amphibians, and mammals on a yearly, seasonal, or weekly basis (RONS 94001). Study the impact of water management practices on these species. Studies should include; snowy plover (RONS 94007), endemic snails (RONS 97004), barking frogs (RONS 97002), velvet ants (mutilids) (RONS 96001), Fish (RONS 94010), butterflies (RONS 97001), dragonflies, and grasshoppers (RONS 97003).

2:    Provide food, habitat and feeding areas for wintering bird populations (e.g., shore and marsh birds, and waterfowl) by manipulating water levels in impoundments (flooding and draw down regiments) and by producing agricultural crops on federal lands. Farm an additional 100 acres of farmland for waterfowl food production (RONS 91023) and construct required buildings and install needed wells to support the farming effort (RONS 91009 and 91021) by 2008.

3:    Promote research of lesser known native species, typically amphibians, reptiles, small mammals, invertebrates, and native vegetation. Address potential hazards from zebra mussels and other exotic invasions.

4:    Promote education in area schools and NGOs on the value of the short-grass prairie ecosystem by conducting interpretive talks, providing four field days per year for school and NGO groups, upgrading the 8-mile auto tour route to include educational displays and brochures, and promoting research projects with area universities addressing problems wildlife and landowners face in the Pecos Valley.

5:    By the year 2002 and in coordination with the North American Waterfowl Management Plan/ Central Flyway Objectives, assist with the revision and completion of the Pecos Valley Waterfowl Management Plan to reflect conformance to the Goals and Objectives of this document.

Objective 3: Following existing recovery plan objectives manage, monitor and study threatened, endangered, and candidate species (Appendix I), their habitat requirements, predator susceptibility, exotic species encroachment and human-induced impacts to prevent further decline and eventual loss.

Strategies

1: Assess and monitor current population dynamics, habitat preference, use and availability, and distribution on federal lands. Studies conducted should include a habitat and species survey for the least shrew (RONS 97009).

2: Provide protected habitat free from disturbance (e.g., all terrain vehicles, hunting, aircraft, trampling, etc.) as required to protect sensitive species on a case by case basis through opportunistic management practices such as temporary or seasonal road closures.

3: Support education about local endangered species exist for area schools, and NGO's by conducting informative talks, upgrading auto tour routes on federal lands to include educational displays and brochures, and promoting research of habitat requirements, population dynamics and problems endangered and threatened wildlife face in the Pecos Ecosystem.

4: Maintain a clearing house on information regarding species of question, providing technical and informative support for other agencies and private land owners. Participate as a control site for the assessment of potential biological control of salt cedar with the U. S. Department of Agriculture (USDA).

Objective 4: Utilize appropriate fire management to protect human life and property in and adjacent to the refuge while maintaining or mimicking natural ecosystem processes. Fire management will comprise approximately 20% of the total annual habitat management capabilities on the Refuge.

Strategies

1: Implement the Bitter Lake NWR and Dexter National Fish Hatchery (Pecos Fire Management Complex) Fire Management Plan within one year.

2: Conduct a fire prevention program in cooperation with other agencies.

3: Suppress all wildfire on the refuge and within the wilderness, in an efficient, cost effective manner, while minimizing environmental impacts from unwarranted suppression activities.

4: Utilize prescribed burning to create favorable habitat conditions required by all forms of native wildlife.

5: By 2003 construct a basic headquarters building on the Refuge to house the fire crew and equipment (RONS 97008).

Objective 5: Acquire appropriate land parcels as they become available to ensure the protection of habitat and continuity of management efforts along the Pecos River drainage. Proposed acquisition parcels range from approximately 10 to 2,500 acres in size (Appendix J, Figure 6).

Strategies

1: Pursue acquisition of land parcels on a willing seller basis as designated on the proposed land acquisition map (Appendix J, Figure 6).

2: Secure important habitat through fee or easement acquisitions on a willing seller basis.

5.2 Hydrological Restoration and Water Quality

Goal 2: **To restore and maintain a hydrological system that mimics the natural processes along the Pecos River drainage by: (1) restoration of the channel, as well as restoration of threatened, endangered and special concern species; and (2) control of exotic species and manage trust responsibilities for maintenance of plant and animal communities and to satisfy traditional recreational demands.**

Objective 1: Restore a more natural stream morphology and flood plain geometry to the 15 mile reach of the Pecos River within the Refuge in order to benefit native aquatic and riparian plant and animal communities.

Strategies

1: Develop communication and cooperation with ongoing projects within the basin that affect channel morphology, including the Pecos River Native Riparian Restoration Project, Soil Conservation Service (SCS), Army Corps of Engineers (Corp), Bureau of Reclamation (BOR) and the Bureau of Land Management.

2: Define changes to the hydro graph and channel morphology that have occurred within the last 75 years using US Geological Survey flow records, SCS aerial photographs, and other historic records. Determine the restoration potential within the confines of irrigation demands and flood control concerns.

3: Work with the BOR and associated State and Irrigation Agencies to have reservoir releases mimic the natural hydrograph of the River. The mimicry of the natural hydrograph should restore peak flows, within flood control concerns, and shape releases, both allowing for the sculpting of the channel and reactivation of the flood plain.

4: By 2008 restore 1,000 acres of the pre-1940 channel geometry to the Pecos River within the confines of the Bitter Lake National Wildlife Refuge (RONS 96012).

5: By 2001 restore 100 acres of habitat associated with 25 gypsum sinkholes by filling in the connecting trenches constructed in the 1940's. This activity will protect the integrity of individual sinkholes and their representative species composition (RONS 94090) due to a steadily rising water table in the past few years.

6: By 2003 develop and manage 60 acres as "moist soil units" by converting non-productive farm fields to seasonal wetlands on Middle Tract to provide food and habitat for waterfowl and a variety of other species (RONS 96003).

7: Increase public awareness of the benefits of a naturally mimicked hydro graph and natural channel morphology restoration. Use the Refuge as an education center for this campaign.

8: Conduct a long-term contaminant monitoring program on the refuge .

9: Conduct continuous management of existing wetlands, impoundments, marshes, and support canals for optimal management of fish and wildlife (RONS 94011). By the year 2000 purchase a trailer to haul existing excavation equipment to allow more efficient use on habitat management projects (RONS 97005).

10: Conduct monthly water level monitoring as required in agreement between the Service and Department of Justice for the five year period ending in August of 2001(RONS 97010) and conduct a study to determine the water level changes in the sinkholes and in Bitter Creek (RONS 96006).

51

Objective 2: Restore populations of aquatic species designated as endangered, threatened, or of special concern to a sustainable level. Aquatic species in these categories include green throat darter, Pecos gambusia, Pecos bluntnose shiner, Pecos pupfish, Mexican tetra, Pecos assiminea, Kosters tyronia, Roswell spring snail, Knoels amphipod, and Pecos sunflower.

Strategies

1: Develop cooperative management strategies with other federal, state and non-governmental agencies (NGOs) to support maintenance and restoration of habitats supporting (or potentially supporting) native communities, with special emphasis on federal and state listed species.

2: Assist in developing, within 18 months of listing or revise at 5-year intervals, Recovery Plans for listed species (Appendix I).

3: Assist in conducting status surveys of Notice of Review species and prepare reports that detail range reductions, reasons for decline, and recommended conservation measures.

4: Participate to the extent possible in conducting studies under a "Memorandum of Understanding" with the Service, BOR, New Mexico Department of Game and Fish (NMDGF), Carlsbad Irrigation District, and the New Mexico Office of the State Engineer regarding the impact of reservoir operations on Pecos bluntnose shiner, as well as the entire fish community, between Santa Rosa Dam and Brantley Reservoir.

5: Promote a public outreach campaign that stresses the importance of restoring endangered species in the Pecos River Basin and their relation to sound ecosystem management.

6: Provide study sites to support life history research on the Pecos pupfish, and introduce the Pecos pupfish to into sinkhole W3 (Appendix J, Figure 2.) by September 30, 1998.. Continue evaluating other isolated Refuge wetlands as potential refugia and conduct annual monitoring of populations of pupfish in six impoundments during late summer and early fall to check for invasion of sheepshead minnow.

7: Construct an adequate concrete fish barrier at the South Weir of the Refuge by September 30, 1998.

Objective 3: Develop and support ongoing resource management tactics that emphasize the control of up to 5,000 acres annually of non-native plant species and to reduce or eliminate to the degree possible, populations of non-native animal species (excepting non-native game species).

Strategies

1: Work with NMDGF to monitor the effects of all introduced game-fish stockings on native communities. Those fisheries determined to have significant, negative impacts to native fishes and/or invertebrates should be eliminated or significantly reduced.

2: Assist NMDGF in eliminating future incidental introductions of non-native fishes to the Pecos River, its tributaries, or other water bodies with potential access to these streams.

3: By 2003 construct a concrete fish barrier on Salt Creek to protect populations of native pupfish by preventing upstream movement of exotic fish from the Pecos River (RONS 94014).

4: Control salt cedar and other non-native vegetation from riparian areas of the Pecos River and its tributaries.

5: Initiate control measures for restoration of native riparian plant communities along the Pecos River, Bitter Creek and associated springs and sink holes located within Bitter Lake National Wildlife Refuge.

6: Participate to the extent possible, in cooperating with the USDA or other organizations in approved biological control efforts toward control of exotic salt cedar. The Refuge will provide test study sites when practical.

7: Utilize all interactions with the public (i.e., media releases, public meetings, etc.) to disseminate information on the negative impacts that most non-native species have on native species and the natural ecosystem as a whole.

Objective 4: Continue to manage trust responsibilities for maintenance of plant and animal communities and to satisfy traditional recreational demands.

Strategies

1: Develop, implement, and maintain an integrated approach with cooperators (Indian tribes, state wildlife conservation departments, other federal agencies, local governments, soil and water conservation districts, private landowners) to identify trust resources and implement/maintain management practices for management of native and non-native plant and animal communities.

2: Conduct continuous evaluations of federal actions impacting plant and animal communities based upon requirements of the Fish and Wildlife Coordination Act, the National Environmental Policy Act, and other federal laws and regulations .

3: Use local media to identify, promote, and gather support for maintaining trust responsibilities that are integrated with other resource management issues.

5.3 Public Use, Recreation, and Wildlife Interpretation & Education

GOAL 3: **To offer compatible wildlife-dependent public access and recreational opportunities to include compatible forms of hunting, wildlife observation and photography, and continue wildlife interpretation and educational efforts.**

Objective 1: Working with NMDGF to improve existing compatible waterfowl and crane hunting opportunities at Bitter Lake NWR in the Middle Tract, and continue to allow hunting in the North Tract to include deer, rabbits, ducks, geese, coots, cranes, dove, quail, and pheasant.

Strategies

1: Use local media and other public outreach tools to educate the public and enhance wildlife-dependent recreational experiences including hunting on the refuge.

2: Continue to improve consistencies between federal and state regulations on wildlife areas.

Objective 2: Develop improved compatible recreational opportunities for wildlife viewing and photography at Bitter Lake NWR to allow for as many as 70,000 visitors annually.

Strategies

1: Improve wildlife viewing opportunities through road reconstruction and upgrading to an all-weather road for the wildlife tour route (RONS 960099) by 2005.

54

2: Construct a new information and tour route sign at the tour registration building (RONS 96005), and incorporate six interpretative signs into the two raised wildlife overlooks (RONS 96002) by 1999.

3: Use local media and public outreach to educate the public about opportunities for wildlife viewing and photography at Bitter Lake NWR.
Within one year install a new educational exhibit at the visitor reception area of the Refuge headquarters (RONS 96010), and generate a new up-to-date brochure and make it available to the public (RONS 96004).

4: By 2003 generate and make available to the public a new brochure about the endangered and threatened fish species on the Refuge and how the Refuge plays a critical role in the protection of these species (RONS 94013).

5: Within four years designate and develop a wheel chair accessible wildlife viewing trail near the Refuge headquarters to allow additional wildlife viewing (RONS 94015).

6: By 2008 design and install up to four shade ramadas using natural rock or brick facing to allow screened viewing of wildlife utilizing Refuge ponds (RONS 94017).

7: By 2008 construct a new wheel chair accessible restroom facility at the Refuge Headquarters (RONS 91020).

8: Work with New Mexico Highway Department to properly place directional signs along the Highway 70 bypass at Pine Ridge Road.

9: Construct an interpretive panel, and stop over view point at the Salt Creek Wilderness boundary in cooperation with the New Mexico Highway Department.

10: Arrange for placement of signs at mile marker 161 on Highway 380 as part of a cooperative agreement with New Mexico Highway Department.

5.4 Cultural Resources

GOAL 4:. To protect and maintain cultural resources on the Bitter Lake NWR for the benefit of present and future generations.

> **Objective 1:** Fully identify and evaluate historical cultural resources on the Bitter Lake NWR in order to allow for their preservation.

Strategies

1: Working with the State Historical Preservation Officer (SHPO) and other interested partners complete a survey and inventory of cultural resources on Bitter Lake NWR by 2003. Conduct and investigation of up to ten archaeological sites in the uplands of the Refuge to survey and document the existence and condition of the cultural resource sites (RONS 98001).

2: Based upon the results of the cultural resources survey and inventory develop and implement a protection and enhancement plan for the cultural resources on Bitter Lake NWR within three years of the survey and inventory completion.

3: Use local media to educate and inform the public about the nature and value of cultural resources present on Bitter Lake NWR.

4: Construct a one-mile long barbed wire fence to limit vehicle access on the east side of the northern tract of the Refuge (RONS 96007) by 1999.

5.5 Interagency Coordination and Relations

GOAL 5: To strengthen interagency and jurisdictional relationships in order to coordinate efforts with respect to refuge and surrounding area issues, resulting in decisions benefiting fish and wildlife resources, while at the same time avoiding duplication of effort.

Objective 1: Develop interagency and jurisdictional relationships that will help control and prevent encroachment on Refuge lands and habitat.

Strategies

1: Develop agreements with BLM and other stakeholders that will define and implement policies and requirements (such as Environmental Impact Statements (EIS) for gas exploration adjacent to the Refuge within three years.

2: Develop a stronger relationship with local agencies, landowners, the county, and other stakeholders, to control land development adjacent to the refuge in a way that will benefit wildlife .

5.6 Improvement of Staffing and Funding

GOAL 6: **To effect improvements to staffing and funding that will result in long-term enhancement of habitat and wildlife resources in the area of ecological concern, and allow the achievement of the goals of this plan and the goals of the National Wildlife Refuge System.**

Objective 1: Increase staffing to the proposed "Full Staffing Level" or its equivalent in order to provide the level of effort needed to accomplish the goals of this plan (Appendix L.).

1: Utilize internal mechanisms such as The Refuge Operating Needs System (RONS) to justify and acquire the additional funding and personnel to accomplish the Refuge goals within ten years.

2: Pursue agreements with other interested agencies and public partners to provide the needed personnel and funds to accomplish the Refuge goals.

3: Evaluate the need and feasibility of contracting firms to conduct portions of the work needed to accomplish the refuge goals.

4: As a priority to allow accomplishment of public education and recreation objectives and strategies, effect authorization for an Outdoor Recreation Planner position (RONS 96008) within one year.

5: Build a workforce of dedicated and motivated individuals who will cost-effectively manage fish , wildlife and their habitats.

6.0 BITTER LAKE MANAGEMENT STRATEGIES BY TRACT

This section contains the strategies that unless otherwise noted in the text, are site specific to the respective management tracts of Bitter lake NWR.

6.1 North Tract (Salt Creek Wilderness)

Strategies

1: The Refuge will continue to manage the Salt Creek Wilderness in accordance with the existing wilderness goals reflected in this document. In accordance with the Wilderness Act of 1964, no vehicular access will be allowed. For access by mineral right (oil and gas) and leaseholders the manager is required to provide "reasonable" access. That access will be determined on a case-by-case basis. Prior to issuance of a permit to enter the wilderness for legitimate proposed development of oil, gas, or mineral rights, the manager will require from the owner of the rights a detailed plan to include the rationale necessary for the use of motorized or mechanized equipment, the scope and duration of development, and a mitigation plan in the event surface resources including access ways are disturbed.

2: By 2003 construct a concrete fish barrier on Salt Creek to protect populations of native pupfish by preventing upstream movement of exotic fish from the Pecos River (RONS 94014).

3: Construct a one-mile long barbed wire fence to limit vehicle access on the east side of the northern tract of the Refuge (RONS 96007) by 1999.

4: Monitor wildlife populations including neotropical migrants (e.g., passerine, shore and marsh birds, and waterfowl), reptile and amphibians, and mammals on a yearly, seasonal, or weekly basis (RONS 94001). Study the impact of water management practices on these species. Studies should include; snowy plover (RONS 94007), endemic snails (RONS 97004), barking frogs (RONS 97002), velvet ants (mutilids) (RONS 96001), Fish (RONS 94010), butterflies (RONS 97001), dragonflies, and grasshoppers (RONS 97003).

6.2 Middle Tract

Strategies

1: Improve wildlife viewing opportunities through road reconstruction and upgrading to an all-weather road for the wildlife tour route (RONS 96009) within seven years.

2: Construct a new information and tour route sign at the tour registration building (RONS 96005), and incorporate six interpretative signs into the two raised wildlife overlooks (RONS 96002) by 1999 (one of the overlooks is located on the south tract).

3: Use local media and public outreach to educate the public about opportunities for wildlife viewing and photography at Bitter Lake NWR.
Within two years install a new educational exhibit at the visitor reception area of the Refuge headquarters (RONS 96010), and generate a new up-to-date brochure and make it available to the public (RONS 96004, the brochures will be distributed on the middle tract).

4: By 2003 generate and make available to the public a new brochure about the endangered and threatened fish species on the Refuge and how the Refuge plays a critical role in the protection of these species (RONS 94013, the brochures will be distributed on the middle tract).

5: Within four years designate and develop a wheel chair accessible wildlife viewing trail near the Refuge headquarters to allow additional wildlife viewing (RONS 94015).

6: By 2008 design and install up to four shade ramadas using natural rock or brick facing to allow screened viewing of wildlife utilizing Refuge ponds (RONS 94017).

7: By 2008 construct a new wheel chair accessible restroom facility at the Refuge Headquarters (RONS 91020).

8: By 2008 restore 1,000 acres of the pre-1940 channel geometry to the Pecos River within the confines of the Bitter Lake National Wildlife Refuge (RONS 96012).

9: By 2001 restore 100 acres of habitat associated with 25 gypsum sinkholes by filling in the connecting trenches constructed in the 1940's. This activity will protect the integrity of individual sinkholes and their representative species composition (RONS 96009).

10: By 2003 develop and manage 60 acres as "moist soil units" by converting non-productive farm fields to seasonal wetlands on the Middle Tract to provide food and habitat for waterfowl and a variety of other species (RONS 96003).

11: Conduct monthly water level monitoring as required in agreement between the Service and Department of Justice for the five year period ending in August of 2001 (RONS 97010) and conduct a study to determine the water level changes in the sinkholes and in Bitter Creek (RONS 96006).

12: Conduct continuous management of existing wetlands, impoundments, marshes, and support canals for optimal management of fish and wildlife (RONS 94011). By the year 2000 purchase a trailer to haul existing excavation equipment to allow more efficient use on habitat management projects (RONS 97005).

13: By 2003 construct a basic headquarters building on the Refuge to house the fire crew and equipment (RONS 97008).

14: Preserve 65 acres of upland habitat through bank erosion control of the Pecos River (RONS 91010) by 2003 (portions of the habitat are located on both the middle and south tracts).

15: Restore 250 acres in the Research Natural Areas and 1,000 acres in other sections of the Refuge by removal and control of exotic salt cedar (RONS 96011, 94002, and 94005) by 2003.

16: Restore 10 acres of upland habitat near the Refuge headquarters by planting native overstory vegetation and providing appropriate irrigation (RONS 94003) by the year 2000.

17: Reseed 140 acres of abandoned fields that is too alkali for crop production with native alkali sacaton and manage the area as native grasslands (RONS 94008) by 2003 (portions of the farm fields are on the middle and south tract).

18: Monitor wildlife populations including neotropical migrants (e.g., passerine, shore and marsh birds, and waterfowl), reptile and amphibians, and mammals on a yearly, seasonal, or weekly basis (RONS 94001). Study the impact of water management practices on these species. Studies should include; snowy plover (RONS 94007), endemic snails (RONS 97004), barking frogs (RONS 97002), velvet ants (mutilids) (RONS 96001), Fish (RONS 94010), butterflies (RONS 97001), dragonflies, and grasshoppers (RONS 97003).

19:    Working with the State Historical Preservation Officer (SHPO) and other interested partners complete a survey and inventory of cultural resources on Bitter Lake NWR by 2003. Conduct and investigation of up to ten archaeological sites in the uplands of the Refuge to survey and document the existence and condition of the cultural resource sites (RONS 98001).

6.3   South Tract

Strategies

1:    Provide food, habitat and feeding areas for wintering bird populations (e.g., shore and marsh birds, and waterfowl) by manipulating water levels in impoundments (flooding and draw down regiments) and by producing agricultural crops on federal lands. Farm an additional 100 acres of farmland for waterfowl food production (RONS 91023) and construct required buildings and install needed wells to support the farming effort (RONS 91009 and 91021) by 2008.

2:    Reseed 140 acres of abandoned farm fields that is to alkali for crop production with native alkali sacaton and manage the area as native grasslands (RONS 94008) by the year 2000.

3:    Restore 10 acres of cropland through treatment to remove noxious johnson grass on the ten acres (RONS 94004) by the year 2001.

4:    Preserve 65 acres of upland habitat through bank erosion control of the Pecos River (RONS 91010) by 2003.

7.0 REFERENCES

United States Fish and Wildlife Service. 1994. Bitter Lake National Wildlife Refuge Annual Narrative Report Calender Year 1994. Bitter Lake National Wildlife Refuge. [15]

United States Fish and Wildlife Service. 1996. Bitter Lake National Wildlife Refuge Annual Narrative Report Calender Year 1996. Bitter Lake National Wildlife Refuge.[15]

United States Fish and Wildlife Service. 1997. Fire Management Plan Bitter Lake National Wildlife Refuge Dexter National Fish Hatchery (Pecos Fire Management Complex)January 1997. Bitter Lake National Wildlife Refuge.[15]

United States Fish and Wildlife Service. 1981. Bitter Lake National Wildlife Refuge Salt Creek Wilderness, Wilderness Management Plan, January 1981. Bitter Lake National Wildlife Refuge.[15]

United States Fish and Wildlife Service. 1994. Pecos River Ecosystem Plan 1994. U. S. Fish and Wildlife Service, Region 2, Albuquerque, New Mexico.

United States Fish and Wildlife Service. 1996. Recovery Plan for the interior population of the Least tern (Sterna antillarum) January 1996. U. S. Fish and Wildlife Service, Twin Cities , Minnesota.

United States Fish and Wildlife Service. 1992. Pecos Bluntnose Shiner recovery Plan. U. S. Fish and Wildlife Service, Region 2, Albuquerque, New Mexico. 57 pp.

United States Fish and Wildlife Service. 1982. Pecos Gambusia (Gambusia nobilis) recovery Plan. U. S. Fish and Wildlife Service, Albuquerque, New Mexico. iii +41 pp.

DeGraaf, R.M. and Rappole, J. H. 1995. Neotropical Migratory Birds, (Natural History, Distribution, and Population Change) Comstock Publishing Associates, a Division of Cornell University Press, Ithaca and London.

Ehrlich, Paul R., D.S. Dobkin and D.Wheye. 1988. The Birders Handbook: a Field Guide to the Natural History of North American Birds. Simon and Schuster.

Field Guide to the Birds of North America, National Geographic Society.1987.

Peterson, R.T. 1961. A Field Guide to Western Birds. Houghton Mifflin Co. Boston.

Udvardy, M.D.F. 1977. The Audubon Society Field Guide to North American Birds (Western Region). Alfred A. Knopf, Inc. New York.

---

[15] Internal Administrative Guidance Document.

Burt, W.H. and R.P.Grossenheider, 1976. A Field Guide to the Mammals. Houghten Mifflin Co. Boston.

Arnberger, L.P. 1982. Flowers of the Southwest Mountains. Southwest Parks and Monuments Association.

Brockman, C.F. 1986. Trees of North America. Golden Press. New York.

Elmore, F.H. 1976. Shrubs and Trees of the Southwest Uplands. Southwest Parks and Monuments Association.

Hitchcock, A.H. 1971. Manual of Grasses of the United States. Volume One. Dover Publications, Inc. New York.

Whitney, S. 1985. Western Forests. The Audubon Society Nature Guides. Alfred A. Knopf, Inc. New York.

Rickett, H.W. 1966. Wild Flowers of the United States. Vol 4. Part 1. McGraw-Hill Book Co. New York.

Whitson, T.D., L.C. Burrill, S.A. Dewey, D. Cudney, B.E. Nelson, R.D. Lee, R.Parker. 1991 Weeds of the West. Western Society of Weed Science. Pioneer of Jackson Hole, Publ.

MacMahon, James A., 1992. The Audubon Society Nature Guides. Deserts. Alfred A. Knopf, Inc. New York.

Stebbins, Robert C. 1985. A Field Guide to Western Reptiles and Amphibians. Houghton Mifflin Co. Boston.

Eddy, Samuel. 1969. How to Know the Fresh Water Fishes. Wm. C. Brown Company. Debuque, Iowa.

Pennak, Robert W. 1953. Fresh-Water Invertebrates of the United States. Roland Press Company. New York.

8.0 LIST OF PREPARERS

Research Management Consultants, Inc. (RMCI)

Louis J. Bridges- Project Scientist/Biologist

> B.S. Biology /Natural History; M. A. Science Education
> Six years of experience at RMCI as an Environmental Scientist/Biologist. 15 years of related experience ranging from research with the Colorado Division of Wildlife to Environmental Science Instructor at the University of Northern Colorado.

J. Paul Wharry- Environmental Scientist III

> B.A. Biology
> Six years of experience at RMCI as an Environmental Scientist. 15 years of related experience ranging from High School Science Instructor to Director of the Frontiers of Science Institute at the University of Northern Colorado.

Contributors

Thomas P. Baca, Senior Natural Resources Planner, Division of Refuges

> M. A. Public Administration
> Seven years experience in developing Comprehensive Conservation Plans for National Wildlife Refuges in Region 2. Four years experience as Region 2 Wilderness Coordinator. Four years experience, U. S. Senate Staff, Natural Resource and Transportation Issues.

William R. Radke, Refuge Manager Bitter Lake National Wildlife Refuge

> B. S. Wildlife Ecology
> Five years experience as Refuge Manager for Bitter Lake NWR. Eleven years experience as a Wildlife Biologist for U.S. Fish and Wildlife Service at other refuges.

Appendix A
Butterflies of Bitter Lake NWR

Butterflies Documented on and Adjacent to Bitter Lake NWR, Roswell, NM.

Hesperiidae - Skippers

Erynnis brizo	Banded oak dusky wing
Erynnis funeralis	Streamlined Duskywing
Pyrgus communis	Checkered skipper
Pholisora catullus	Common sooty wing
Hesperopsis alpheus	Saltbush Sootywing
Copaeodes aurantiacus	Western tiny skipper
Atalopedes campestris	Sachem skipper
Amblyscirtes nysa	Mottled Little Skipper
Amblyscirtes eos	Dotted Little skipper

Papilionidae - Swallowtails

Papilio philenor	Pipevine swallowtail
Papilio polyxenes asterius	Black swallowtail
Papilio cresphontes	Giant swallowtail
Papilio multicaudatus	Two-tailed swallowtail

Pieridae - Whites and Sulfurs

Pieris protodice	Checkered white
Pieris rapae	Cabbage white
Colias philodice	Common sulfur
Colias eurytheme	Orange sulfur
Zerene cesonia	Southern dogface
Phoebis sennae	Cloudless sulfur
Eurema mexicanum	Mexican yellow
Eurema nicippe	Sleepy sulfur
Nathalis iole	Dwarf sulfur

Lycaenidae - Hairstreaks and Blues

Strymon melinus	Gray hairstreak
Brephidium exile	Western pygmy blue
Leptotes marina	Marine blue
Hemiargus isola	Reakirt's blue
Plebejus melissa	Orange-bordered blue

Libytheidae - Snout Butterflies

Libytheana bachmanii larvata	Snout Butterfly

Nymphalidae - Brush-Footed Butterflies

Dione vanillae	Gulf fritillary
Euptoita claudia	Variegated fritillary
Chlosyne leanira fulvia	Paintbrush Checkerspot
Chlosyne lacinia crocale	Sunflower patch
Chlosyne definita	Chihuahua patch
Phyciodes texanus	Texas Crescent
Phyciodes vesta	Mesquite Crescent
Phyciodes tharos tharos	Pearl Crescent
Phyciodes pictus	Painted crescent
Polygonia interrogationis	Questionmark
Nymphalis antiopa	Mourning Cloak
Vanessa virginiensis	American Painted Lady
Vanessa cardui	Painted Lady

*Vanessa annabella**	West Coast Lady
*Vanessa atalanta**	Red admiral
Precis coenia	Buckeye
Junonia nigrosuffusa	Dark buckeye
Limenitis arcchippus obsoleta	Viceroy
Limenitis bredowii	Sister
*Anaea andria**	Goatweed Butterfly

Danaidae - Milkweed Butterflies

*D. plexippus**	Monarch
*D. gilippus strigosus**	Desert queen

* Denotes species represented by specimen in refuge collection.

Appendix B
Dragonflies and Damselflies of Bitter Lake NWR

Partial List of Bitter Lake NWR Odonata (dragonflies)

(Anisoptera)
Gomphidae
  Progomphus borealis
  Phyllogomphoides stigmatus
  Gomphus militaris
  Gomphus (Gomphurus) externus
  Stylurus intricatus
  Erpetogomphus diadophis
Aeshnidae
  Anax amazili
  Anax junius
  Anax walsinghami
  Oplonaeshna armata
  Aeshna multicolor
  Coryphaeschna luteipennis
Corduliidae
  Macromia annulata
  Epitheca petechialis
Libellulidae
  Macrodiplax balteata
  Orthemis ferruginea
  Perithemis mooma or tenera
  Pseudoleon superbus
  Libellula quadrimaculata
  Libellula comanche
  Libellula luctuosa
  Libellula odiosa
  Libellula composita
  Libellula forensis
  (Plathemis) Libellula lydia
  Libellula pulchella
  Libellula saturata
  (Plathemis) Libellula subornata
  Libellula flavida
  Libellula croceipennis
  Erythrodiplax berenice
  Erythrodiplax connata
  Erythrodiplax minuscula
  Erythrodiplax umbrata
  (Tarnetrum) Sympetrum corruptum
  (Tarnetrum) Sympetrum illotum
  Erythemis collocata
  Erythemis simplicicollis
  (Lepthemis) Erythemis vesiculosa
  Pachydiplax longipennis
  Dythemis fugax
  Dythemis velox
  Paltothemis lineatipes
  Tramea lacerata
  Tramea onusta
  Pantala flavescens
  Pantala hymenaea

Appendix C
Mutilids (Velvet Ants) of Bitter Lake NWR

Velvet Ant (Mutillidae) Species Documented on Bitter Lake NWR, Roswell, NM

Species
Dasymutilla bioculata
Dasymutilla birkmani
Dasymutilla calorata
Dasymutilla caneo
Dasymutilla chiron ursula
Dasymutilla creusa
Dasymutilla digressa
Dasymutilla dugesii
Dasymutilla gorgon
Dasymutilla hispidaria
Dasymutilla klugii
Dasymutilla leda
Dasymutilla nigricauda
Dasymutilla quadriguttata
Dasymutilla scaevola
Dasymutilla snoworum
Dasymutilla stevensii
Dasymutilla texanella
Dasymutilla vesta
Dasymutilla vesta (hybrid)
Dasymutilla vesta errans
Dasymutilla vesta vesta
Dasymutilla vestita
Dasymutilla waco
Undescribed *Dasymutilla* sp.

Myrmilloides grandiceps

Photopsis ceres
Photopsis marpesia

Pseudomethoca bequaterti
Pseudomethoca contumeliosa
Pseudomethoca oceola
Pseudomethoca paludata
Pseudomethoca propinqua

Timulla navasota coahuila
Timulla oajoca
Timulla suspensa sonora
Timulla vagans vagans

Sphaeropthalminae sp.

Typhoctes peculiaris

Appendix D
Fish of Bitter Lake NWR

Family Lepisosteidae - Gars
Longnose gar   *Lepisosteus osseus*

Family Clupeidae - Shads
Gizzard shad   *Dorosoma cepedianum*

Family Characidae - Characins
Mexican tetra   *Astyanax mexicanus*

Family Cyprinidae - Carps and Minnows
Red shiner   *Cyprinella lutrensis*
Common carp   *Cyprinus carpio*
Roundnose minnow   *Dionda episcopa*
Speckled chub   *Extrarius aestivalis*
Plains minnow   *Hybognathus placitus*
Arkansas River shiner   *Notropis girardi*
Rio Grande shiner   *Notropis jemezanus*
Pecos bluntnose shiner   *Notropis simus pecosensis*
Fathead minnow   *Pimephales promelas*

Family Catostomidae - Suckers
River carpsucker   *Carpoides carpio*

Family Ictaluridae - Catfishes
Channel catfish   *Ictalurus punctatus*

Family Cyprinodontidae - Pupfish
Pecos pupfish   *Cyprinodon pecosensis*

Family Fundulidae - Killifishes
Plains killifish   *Fundulus zebrinus*
Rainwater killifish   *Lucania parva*

Family Poeciliidae - Livebearers
Mosquitofish   *Gambusia affinis*
Pecos gambusia   *Gambusia nobilis*

Family Atherinidae - Silversides
Inland silversides   *Menidia beryllina*

Family Centrarchidae - Sunfishes
Green sunfish   *Lepomis cyanellus*
White crappie   *Pomoxis annularis*

Family Percidae - Perches
Walleye   *Stizostedion vitreum*
Greenthroat darter   *Etheostoma lepidum*

Appendix E
Amphibians and Reptiles of Bitter Lake NWR

Amphibians and Reptiles Documented at Bitter Lake NWR, Chaves County, NM

Family Ambystomatidae - Mole Salamanders
    Tiger salamander   *Ambystoma tigrinum*

Family Leptodactylidae - Tropical Frogs
    Eastern barking frog   *Eleutherodactylus augusti latrans*

Family Pelobatidae - Spadefoot Toads
    Couch's spadefoot toad   *Scaphiopus couchii*
    New Mexico spadefoot toad   *Spea multiplicata*
    Plains spadefoot toad   *Spea bombifrons*

Family Bufonidae - Toads
    Woodhouse's toad   *Bufo woodhousii*
    Red-spotted toad   *Bufo punctatus*
    Great Plains toad   *Bufo cognatus*
    Texas toad   *Bufo speciosus*
    Western green toad   *Bufo debilis insidior*

Family Hylidae - Treefrogs
    Northern cricket frog   *Acris crepitans blanchardi*

Family Ranidae - True Frogs
    Plains leopard frog   *Rana blairi*

Family Chelydridae - Snapping Turtles
    Common snapping turtle   *Chelydra serpentina*

Family Kinosternidae - Mud Turtles
    Yellow mud turtle   *Kinosternon flavescens*

Family Emydidae - Box and Water Turtles
    Western painted turtle   *Chrysemys picta bellii*
    Red-eared slider   *Trachemys scripta elegans*
    Western river cooter   *Pseudemys gorzugi*
    Ornate box turtle   -   *Terrapene ornata ornata*

Family Trionychidae - Softshell Turtles
    Spiny softshell turtle   *Trionyx spiniferus*

Family Phrynosomatidae - Iguanid Lizards
Lesser earless lizard   *Holbrookia maculata*
Side-blotched lizard   *Uta stansburiana*
Texas horned lizard   *Phrynosoma cornutum*
Round-tailed horned lizard   *Phrynosoma modestum*

Family Crotaphytidae - Collared and Leopard Lizards
Collared lizard   *Crotaphytus collaris*
Leopard lizard   *Gambelia wislizenii*

Family Scincidae - Skinks
Many-lined skink   *Eumeces multivirgatus epipleurotus*
Great Plains skink   *Eumeces obsoletus*

Family Teiidae - Whiptail Lizards
Little striped whiptail lizard   *Cnemidophorus inornatus*
Chihuahuan spotted whiptail   *Cnemidophorus exanguis*
Western whiptail lizard   *Cnemidophorus tigris*
Checkered whiptail lizard   *Cnemidophorus grahamii (tesselatus)*

Family Leptotyphlopidae - Blind Snakes
Texas blind snake   *Leptotyphlops dulcis*

Family Colubridae - Colubrid Snakes
Ringneck snake   *Diadophis punctatus*
Western hognose snake   *Heterodon nasicus*
Yellowbelly racer   *Coluber constrictor*
Coachwhip   *Masticophis flagellum*
Great Plains rat snake   *Elaphe guttata*
Glossy snake   *Arizona elegans*
Bullsnake   *Pituophis melanoleucus*
Desert kingsnake   *Lampropeltis getula splendida*
New Mexico milk snake   *Lampropeltis triangulum celaenops*
Long-nosed snake   *Rhinocheilus lecontei*
Common garter snake   *Thamnophis sirtalis*
Checkered garter snake   *Thamnophis marcianus*
Arid land ribbon snake   *Thamnophis proximus diabolicus*
Ground snake   *Sonora semiannulata*
Western hooknose snake   *Gyalopion canum*
Plains black-headed snake   *Tantilla nigriceps*
Night snake   *Hypsiglena torquata*

Family Viperidae - Rattlesnakes
Desert massasauga   *Sistrurus catenatus*
Western diamondback rattlesnake   *Crotalus atrox*
Prairie rattlesnake   *Crotalus v. viridis*

Appendix F
Birds of Bitter Lake NWR

BIRDS OF BITTER LAKE NWR, CHAVES COUNTY, NEW MEXICO

Bitter Lake NWR contains a mix of natural wetlands, riparian corridors, cropland, impoundments, and desert uplands, providing a variety of habitats for a large diversity of birds, including both eastern and western species. Bird activity continues year-round on the Refuge, offering outstanding opportunitites for bird watchers. Shelter belts and trees at Refuge headquarters serve as hotspots for migrating songbirds, primarily in early May. Spring and late summer are marked by marshbird and shorebird migrations. Fall brings raptor migrations, followed by waterfowl concentrations in winter and early spring. A number of birds nest on the refuge each summer, including unique species such as the snowy plover and the interior least tern.

This list contains 352 species that have been recorded on the refuge through September 1998. (Species are listed in accordance with the Sixth American Ornithologist Union Checklist.) Most birds are migratory, therefore their seasonal occurrence is coded as follows:

SEASON

SP	Spring	March - May
S	Summer	June - July
F	Fall	August - November
W	Winter	December - February

RELATIVE ABUNDANCE

A	Abundant	Very numerous.
C	Common	Likely to be seen or heard in suitable habitat and at the suitable time of day.
U	Uncommon	Present, but not certain to be seen.
O	Occasional	Seen only a few times during a season.
R	Rare	May be present but not every year.
X	Accidental	Has been seen only once or twice.
*		A species known to nest, either currently or historically, on or adjacent to the Refuge.

NOTES   For rare or accidental species, the date the bird was last documented is noted.

	SP	S	F	W	NOTES
LOONS-GREBES					
Red-throated Loon			X		11/57
Arctic Loon			X	X	11/70
Common Loon	R		R	O	
*Pied-billed Grebe	C	U	C	C	
Horned Grebe	R		R	R	
Red-necked Grebe				X	02/55
Eared Grebe	C	R	C	U	
Western Grebe	O	R	O	U	
Clark's Grebe		R	R	R	

PELICANS-CORMORANTS-FRIGATEBIRD

American White Pelican.......	C	O	C	R	
Brown Pelican.....................	X	X	X		07/98
Double-crested Cormorant...	U	R	U	R	
Neotropic Cormorant...........	U	U	O		
Magnificent Frigatebird........			X		10/88

BITTERNS-HERONS-IBISES-SPOONBILL

*American Bittern...............	U	U	U	U	
*Least Bittern.......................	R	R	R		
Great Blue Heron................	C	U	C	C	
Great Egret.........................	O	O	O	O	
*Snowy Egret......................	C	C	C	R	
Little Blue Heron................	R	O	R		
Tricolored Heron................	R	R	R		
Reddish Egret.....................		X	X		09/98
Cattle Egret........................	O	O	R	R	
*Green Heron......................	O	C	U	R	
*Black-crowned Night-Heron	C	C	U	U	
Yellow-crowned Night-Heron	R	R	R		10/95
White Ibis............................			X	X	09/76
White-faced Ibis..................	U	O	U	R	
Roseate Spoonbill................			X		10/83

SWANS-GEESE-DUCKS

Fulvous Whistling-Duck........	R	R	R		08/88
Black-bellied Whistling-Duck				X	12/84
Tundra Swan........................			R	O	
Greater White-fronted Goose	O		O	O	
Snow Goose........................	C	R	A	A	
Ross' Goose........................	C	R	A	A	
*Canada Goose....................	C	U	C	C	
*Wood Duck........................	O	R	O	O	
Green-winged Teal..............	C	U	C	U	
*Mallard..............................	C	C	A	A	
*Northern Pintail..................	A	R	A	C	
Garganey.............................			X		11/86
*Blue-winged Teal...............	C	O	C	O	
*Cinnamon Teal...................	C	C	C	O	
*Northern Shoveler..............	A	U	A	A	
*Gadwall.............................	C	U	C	C	
Eurasian Wigeon	X		X	X	02/97
*American Wigeon...............	A	U	C	A	
*Canvasback........................	U	R	C	C	
Redhead..............................	C	O	C	C	
Ring-necked Duck................	O		U	U	
Greater Scaup......................				X	02/97
*Lesser Scaup......................	U	R	C	C	
Harlequin Duck....................				X	12/77
Oldsquaw.............................	R		R	R	01/97
Surf Scoter.........................	R		R	R	05/96
White-winged Scoter............	R		R	R	01/84
Common Goldeneye.............	O	R	U	U	
Barrow's Goldeneye.............				R	12/56
Bufflehead..........................	C	R	C	C	

Hooded Merganser	R	X	O	O	06/97
Common Merganser	U	R	U	C	
Red-breasted Merganser	O		O	O	
*Ruddy Duck	C	U	C	A	

VULTURES-HAWKS-FALCONS

*Turkey Vulture	C	C	C	X	
Osprey	O	R	O	R	
White-tailed Kite	R	R			07/76
*Mississippi Kite	U	O	R		
Bald Eagle			R	O	
*Northern Harrier	C	U	C	C	
Sharp-shinned Hawk	U	R	U	O	
Cooper's Hawk	U	O	U	U	
Northern Goshawk	R			R	
*Harris' Hawk	R	R	R	R	
*Swainson's Hawk	U	O	U		
Red-tailed Hawk	C	O	C	C	
Ferruginous Hawk	U	R	U	U	
Rough-legged Hawk	O		U	U	
Golden Eagle	O		O	O	
Crested Caracara				X	02/97
*American Kestrel	C	C	C	C	
Merlin	O		O	O	
Peregrine Falcon	O	R	O	R	
Prairie Falcon	U	O	U	U	

PHEASANTS-GROUSE-QUAIL

*Ring-necked Pheasant	C	C	C	C	
Lesser Prairie-Chicken	X		X	X	05/77
*Northern Bobwhite	U	U	U	U	
*Scaled Quail	U	U	U	U	

RAILS-CRANES

Yellow Rail			X	X	08/82
*Virginia Rail	U	U	U	U	
*Sora	U	O	U	U	
Purple Gallinule	X	X			05/55
*Common Moorhen	R	R			
*American Coot	A	C	A	A	
Sandhill Crane	C		A	A	
Common Crane	X				03/61

PLOVERS-SANDPIPERS

Black-bellied Plover	O	R	O	O	
American Golden-Plover	R		R		
*Snowy Plover	C	A	C		
Semipalmated Plover	O	O	O		
*Killdeer	C	C	O		
Mountain Plover	R		R		
*Black-necked Stilt	C	C	U		
*American Avocet	C	C	C	R	
Greater Yellowlegs	C	U	C	U	
Lesser Yellowlegs	C	C	C	R	
Solitary Sandpiper	O	O	O		

Willet	U	O	O		
Spotted Sandpiper	O	O	O	R	
Upland Sandpiper	R		U		
Whimbrel	R				
Long-billed Curlew	U	O	U	R	
Hudsonian Godwit	R	R	R		
Marbled Godwit	O	R	O		
Ruddy Turnstone	X		X		07/98
Red Knot		R	R		
Sanderling	O	O	O		
Semipalmated Sandpiper	O	O	O		
Western Sandpiper	C	C	C	O	
Least Sandpiper	C	C	C	O	
White-rumped Sandpiper	O	O	R		
Baird's Sandpiper	U	U	U		
Pectoral Sandpiper	R	R	R		
Dunlin	O	R	O	R	
Curlew Sandpiper	X				05/96
Stilt Sandpiper	U	U	U		
Buff-breasted Sandpiper		X			06/94
Short-billed Dowitcher	R	R	R		
Long-billed Dowitcher	C	C	C	R	
Common Snipe	U	R	U	U	
Wilson's Phalarope	A	U	U		
Red-necked Phalarope	O		O		

JAEGERS-GULLS-TERNS

Pomarine Jaeger	X			X	12/70
Long-tailed Jaeger		X	X		09/96
Laughing Gull		R			
Franklin's Gull	U	R	U		
Bonaparte's Gull	R		R	R	
Heermann's Gull	X		X		11/76
Ring-billed Gull	C	O	C	C	
Herring Gull	R		O	O	
California Gull			X		08/98
Sabine's Gull			R		08/98
Caspian Tern	R		R		
Common Tern	R		R		
*Forster's Tern	U	U	U		
*Least Tern	U	U	O		
Black Tern	C	U	U		

DOVES-CUCKOO-ROADRUNNER-ANI

Rock Dove	R	R	R	R	
Band-tailed Pigeon		X			06/78
Eurasian Collard Dove		X			07/98
White-winged Dove	O	O	R	R	
*Mourning Dove	A	A	A	C	
Inca Dove	R	R	R	R	
*Yellow-billed Cuckoo	O	O	R		
*Greater Roadrunner	C	C	C	C	
Groove-billed Ani	R	R	R		08/93

OWLS-GOATSUCKERS

*Common Barn Owl	U	U	U	U	
Western Screech-Owl	R	R	R	R	
*Great Horned Owl	C	C	C	C	
*Burrowing Owl	U	U	U	O	
Long-eared Owl	R		R	R	
Short-eared Owl	R		R	R	
Northern Saw-whet Owl	R			R	
Lesser Nighthawk	O	O	O		
*Common Nighthawk	C	C	C		
Common Poorwill	U	O	U		

SWIFTS-HUMMINGBIRDS-KINGFISHER

Chimney Swift	R	R			
White-throated Swift	X				04/59
*Black-chinned Hummingbird	U	U	U		
Calliope Hummingbird		R			
Broad-tailed Hummingbird O	O	O			
Rufous Hummingbird		U	U		
Belted Kingfisher	U	O	U	U	

WOODPECKERS-FLYCATCHERS

Lewis' Woodpecker	R			R	05/72
*Red-headed Woodpecker	O	O	O	R	
Acorn Woodpecker			R		10/72
Red-bellied Woodpecker				X	12/74
Yellow-bellied Sapsucker	R		R	R	
Red-naped Sapsucker	U		U	O	
*Ladder-backed Woodpecker	U	U	U	U	
Downy Woodpecker	O		O	O	
Hairy Woodpecker			R	R	
Northern Flicker	U	R	C	C	
Olive-sided Flycatcher	O	O	O		
Western Wood Pewee	U	U	U		
Willow Flycatcher	R		R		
Dusky Flycatcher	R				
Gray Flycatcher	R				
Cordilleran Flycatcher	R	R			
*Black Phoebe	U	U	U	R	
Eastern Phoebe	R		R	R	
*Say's Phoebe	U	U	U	U	
*Vermilion Flycatcher	O	O	O	R	
*Ash-throated Flycatcher	U	U	U		
Great Crested Flycatcher			X		09/93
Cassin's Kingbird	O		O		
*Western Kingbird	C	C	C		
Eastern Kingbird	R	R	R		09/98
Scissor-tailed Flycatcher	O	R	O		

LARKS-SWALLOWS-JAYS-CROWS

Horned Lark	C	C	C	C	
Purple Martin	R				05/76
Tree Swallow	U	U	U		
Violet-green Swallow	O				
*N. Rough-winged Swallow	C	C	C	R	

Species					Date
Bank Swallow	O	O			
*Cliff Swallow	C	C	C		
Cave Swallow		X			7/97
*Barn Swallow	C	A	C		
Steller's Jay	R		R	R	
*Blue Jay	O	O	O	O	
Western Scrub Jay	R		O	O	
Pinyon Jay	R		R	R	
Clark's Nutcracker			X	X	12/72
*Chihuahuan Raven	C	C	C	R	
Common Raven	R	R	R	R	

NUTHATCHES-WRENS-KINGLETS-GNATCATCHERS

Species					Date
Mountain Chickadee	R		R	R	
Common Bushtit	X				03/71
Red-breasted Nuthatch	O		O	R	
White-breasted Nuthatch	R		R	R	
Pygmy Nuthatch				X	12/70
Brown Creeper	O		O	O	
Cactus Wren	R	R	R	R	
*Rock Wren	U	U	U	U	
Canyon Wren	R			R	
Carolina Wren	X			X	04/73
Bewick's Wren	U		U	U	
House Wren	U		U	O	
Winter Wren			R	R	
Sedge Wren			R	R	
Marsh Wren	C		C	C	
Golden-crowned Kinglet			R	R	
Ruby-crowned Kinglet	C		C	U	
Blue-gray Gnatcatcher	U		U		

THRUSHES-THRASHERS-PIPITS

Species					Date
Eastern Bluebird	R			R	
*Western Bluebird	O	R	O	O	
Mountain Bluebird	O		O	O	
Townsend's Solitaire	R		O	O	
Gray-cheeked Thrush	X				05/67
Hermit Thrush	U		U	R	
Wood Thrush	R		R	R	12/82
*American Robin	O	O	O	O	
Gray Catbird	R	R	R	R	
*Northern Mockingbird	C	C	C	O	
Sage Thrasher	U		U	R	
Brown Thrasher	O	R	R	R	12/96
Bendire's Thrasher		X	X		10/96
*Curve-billed Thrasher	U	U	U	U	
Crissal Thrasher	O	O	O	O	
American Pipit	U		U	C	
Sprague's Pipit	R		U		04/96

WAXWINGS-SILKY FLYCATCHERS-SHRIKES

Cedar Waxwing	U	O	O	O
Phainopepla	R	R	R	R
Northern Shrike	R			R
Loggerhead Shrike	C	U	C	C
European Starling	U	U	U	U

VIREOS-WOOD WARBLERS

Solitary Vireo	U		U		
Warbling Vireo	U	R	U		
Red-eyed Vireo		R	R		10/73
Tennessee Warbler	R				04/73
Orange-crowned Warbler	U		U	R	
Nashville Warbler	O				
Virginia's Warbler	O				05/97
Northern Parula	R	R			05/95
Yellow Warbler	C	R	U		
Chestnut-sided Warbler	X				10/97
Cape May Warbler	X				05/84
Black-throated Blue Warbler	R		R		10/74
Yellow-rumped Warbler	A	O	A	O	
Black-throated Gray Warbler	R		R		
Townsend's Warbler	O	R	O		
Black-throated Green Warbler	R		R		05/96
Yellow-throated Warbler	X		X	X	12/90
Grace's Warbler			X		10/76
Palm Warbler	X				05/71
Bay-breasted Warbler			X		11/80
Black-and-white Warbler	O	R	O		
American Redstart	R		R		05/74
Prothonotary Warbler	X				04/74
Worm-eating Warbler	X				05/98
Ovenbird	R				05/96
Northern Waterthrush	O		R		09/93
Kentucky Warbler	X				04/92
MacGillivray's Warbler	U		U		
*Common Yellowthroat	C	C	U	R	
Wilson's Warbler	C	R	C		
Painted Redstart	X				05/67
Yellow-breasted Chat	U	R	U		

TANAGERS-GROSBEAKS-SPARROWS

Hepatic Tanager	R				05/59
Summer Tanager	U	O	R		
Scarlet Tanager	X				05/74
Western Tanager	U	O	U		
Northern Cardinal	R			R	
Pyrrhuloxia	O	R	O	O	
Rose-breasted Grosbeak	O	R	O		
Black-headed Grosbeak	U	R	U		
Blue Grosbeak	C	C	U		
Lazuli Bunting	U		U		
Indigo Bunting	U	O	U		
Painted Bunting	R		R		
Dickcissel	R	R	R		

Species					
Green-tailed Towhee	U		U	R	
Spotted Towhee	U		U	U	
Canyon Towhee	O	R	O	O	
*Cassin's Sparrow	C	C	C		
Rufous-crowned Sparrow	O		O	O	
American Tree Sparrow	R			O	
Chipping Sparrow	C	C	C	O	
Clay-colored Sparrow	O		U		
Brewer's Sparrow	C		C	U	
Field Sparrow	R		R	R	
Black-chinned Sparrow	R		R		09/94
Vesper Sparrow	U		U	U	
*Lark Sparrow	C	C	C	R	
Black-throated Sparrow	U	U	U	R	
Sage Sparrow	U		U	U	
Lark Bunting	U	U	C	U	
Savannah Sparrow	C		C	C	
Baird's Sparrow	R		R	X	12/97
Grasshopper Sparrow	O		O	R	12/97
Le Conte's Sparrow			R	R	
Fox Sparrow			R	O	
Song Sparrow	C		C	C	
Lincoln's Sparrow	U		U	O	
Swamp Sparrow	U		U	U	
White-throated Sparrow				R	12/76
Golden-crowned Sparrow	X			X	04/70
White-crowned Sparrow	A	O	A	A	
Harris' Sparrow	R			R	05/91
Dark-eyed Junco	C		C	C	
McCown's Longspur	O		O	O	01/97
Chestnut-collared Longspur	C		A	C	

BLACKBIRDS-ORIOLES-FINCHES

Species					
*Red-winged Blackbird	C	C	C	A	
*Eastern Meadowlark	C	C	C	C	
*Western Meadowlark	C	C	C	C	
Yellow-headed Blackbird	U	O	U	O	
Rusty Blackbird			R	R	01/96
Brewer's Blackbird	C	R	C	A	
Great-tailed Grackle	O	O	O	O	
Common Grackle	U	U	U	U	
Bronzed Cowbird	R		R		05/84
*Brown-headed Cowbird	U	U	U	R	
*Orchard Oriole	R	R			05/77
Hooded Oriole	X				05/98
*Bullock's Oriole	C	C	U		
Scott's Oriole	X	X	X		08/96
Purple Finch				X	01/96
Cassin's Finch	R		R	R	
*House Finch	C	C	C	C	
Red Crossbill	X				04/67
Pine Siskin	U		U	O	
Lesser Goldfinch	U		U	R	
American Goldfinch	U		U	U	
Evening Grosbeak	R		R	R	

Appendix G
Mammals of Bitter Lake NWR

Mammals of Bitter Lake NWR, Chaves County, New Mexico

* denotes either an unconfirmed report of a species or a species that may occur but has not been documented.

Family Soricidae - Shrews
Least shrew	*Cryptotis parva*
Desert shrew	*Notiosorex crawfordi*

Family Vespertilionidae - Plain-nose Bats
*Little brown myotis	*Myotis lucifugus*
*Yuma myotis	*Myotis yumanensis*
Cave myotis	*Myotis velifer*
*Long-eared myotis	*Myotis evotis*
*Fringed myotis	*Myotis thysanodes*
*Long-legged myotis	*Myotis volans*
*California myotis	*Myotis californicus*
*Small-footed myotis	*Myotis ciliolabrum*
Silver-haired bat	*Lasionycteris noctivagans*
*Western pipistrelle	*Pipistrellus hesperus*
*Big brown bat	*Eptesicus fuscus*
*Red bat	*Lasiurus borealis*
Hoary bat	*Lasiurus cinereus*
*Spotted bat	*Euderma maculatum*
Townsends big-eared bat	*Plecotus townsendii*
Pallid bat	*Antrozous pallidus*

Family Molossidae - Free-tailed Bats
Brazilian free-tailed bat	*Tadarida brasiliensis*
*Big free-tailed bat	*Nyctinomops macrotis*

Family Leporidae - Rabbits and Hares
Desert cottontail	*Sylvilagus audubonii*
Black-tailed jackrabbit	*Lepus californicus*

Family Sciuridae - Squirrels
Thirteen-lined ground squirrel	*Spermophilus tridecemlineatus*
Mexican ground squirrel	*Spermophilus mexicanus*
Spotted ground squirrel	*Spermophilus spilosoma*
Black-tailed prairie dog	*Cynomys ludovicianus*
Fox squirrel	*Sciurus niger*

Family Geomyidae - Pocket Gophers
Plains pocket gopher	*Geomys bursarius*
Yellow-faced pocket gopher	*Cratogeomys castanops*

Family Heteromyidae - Pocket Mice & Kangaroo Rats
Plains pocket mouse	*Perognathus flavescens*
Silky pocket mouse	*Perognathus flavus*
*Merriam's pocket mouse	*Perognathus merriami*
Hispid pocket mouse	*Chaetodipus hispidus*
Ord's kangaroo rat	*Dipodomys ordii*
*Banner-tailed kangaroo rat	*Dipodomys spectabilis*
Merriam's kangaroo rat	*Dipodomys merriami*

Family Castoridae - Beaver
Beaver   *Castor canadensis*

Family Cricetidae - Rats and Mice

Plains harvest mouse	*Reithrodontomys montanus*
Western harvest mouse	*Reithrodontomys megalotis*
Deer mouse	*Peromyscus maniculatus*
White-footed mouse	*Peromyscus leucopus*
*Brush mouse	*Peromyscus boylei*
Northern grasshopper mouse	*Onychomys leucogaster*
Mearn's grasshopper mouse	*Onychomys arenicola*
Hispid cotton rat	*Sigmodon hispidus*
Southern plains woodrat	*Neotoma micropus*
White-throated woodrat	*Neotoma albigula*
Muskrat	*Ondatra zibethica*

Family Muridae - Old World Rats and Mice

House mouse   *Mus musculus*

Family Erethizontidae - Porcupines

Porcupine   *Erithizon dorsatum*

Family Capramyidae - Nutria

Nutria   *Myocastor coypus*

Family Canidae - Coyotes and Foxes

Coyote	*Canis latrans*
*Swift fox	*Vulpes velox velox*
Kit fox	*Vulpes velox macrotis*
Gray fox	*Urocyon cinereoargenteus*

Family Procyonidae - Raccoon and Ringtail

Ringtail	*Bassariscus astutus*
Raccoon	*Procyon lotor*

Family Mustelidae - Weasel, Badger, Skunks, Otter

Long-tailed weasel	*Mustela frenata*
Black-footed ferret	*Mustela nigripes*
Badger	*Taxidea taxus*
*Western spotted skunk	*Spilogale gracilis*
Striped skunk	*Mephitis mephitis*
*Hog-nosed skunk	*Conepatus mesoleucus*
River Otter	*Lutra canadensis*

Family Felidae - Cats
Bobcat   *Lynx rufus*

Family Suidae - Swine
Feral domestic swine   *Sus scrofa*

Family Cervidae - Deer

Mule deer	*Odocoileus hemionus*
White-tailed deer	*Odocoileus virginianus*

Family Antilocapridae - Pronghorn

Pronghorn   *Antilocapra americana*

Appendix H
Plants of Bitter Lake NWR

NON-FLOWERING PLANTS

Characeae (algae)
Chara hornemannii Wallm.   stonewort, muskgrass
Chara vulgaris L.   stonewort, muskgrass

Ephedranceae (gymnosperms)
Ephedra torreyana Watson   joint-fir, Mormon tea

FLOWERING PLANTS
(Agavaceae: see Lilliaceae)

Aizoaceae
Mollugo verticillata L.   carpetweed
Sesuvium verrucosum Raf.   sea purslane

Amaranthaceae
Amaranthus arenicola I.M. Johnson   sandhills amaranth
Amaranthus crassipes Schlect.   prostrate pigweed
Amaranthus hybtidus L.   green amaranth
Amaranthus palmeri Watson   pigweed
Amaranthus retroflexus L.   redroot pigweed
Amaranthus wrightii Watson   pigweed
Tidestroemia lanuginosa (Nutt.) Standl.,   wooly tidestroemia

Amaryllidiaceae
Zephyranthes longifolia Hemsl.   zephyr-lily

Anacardiaceae
Rhus microphylla Engelm.   desert sumac
Rhus trilobata Nutt. (R. aromatica)   skunk bush, squabush

(Aplaceae: see Umbelliferae)

Apocynaceae
Apocynum cannabinum   Indian hemp

Asclepiadaceae
Asclepias brachystephana Torr.   plains milkweed
Asclepias latifolia (Torr.) Raf.   broadleaf milkweed
Asclepias oenotheroides Cham. & Schlect.   milkweed
Asclepias speciosa Torr.   showy milkweed
Asclepias subverticillata (Gray) Vail   poison milkweed

(Asteraceae: see Compositae.)

Boraginaceae
Cryptantha crassisepala (Torr. & Grne.) Grne.   hiddenflower
Cryptantha jamesii (Torr.) Payson   hiddenflower
Heliotropium convolvulaceum (Nutt.) Gr.   bindweed heliotrope
Heliotropium curassavicum L.   salt heliotrope
Lappula redowskii (Hornem.) Greene   stickseed
Lithospermum incisum Lehm.   gromwell, puccoon

Tiquilia canescens (DC.) A. Richards.   oreja de perro

Tiquilia hispidissima   gyp bush

Cactaceae
Coryphantha macromeris
Echinocactus horizonthalonius Lem.   Turk's head
Echinocactus reichenbachii (Terscheck)   Haage
Echinocactus triglochidiatus Engelm.   claret-cup
Opuntia imbricata (Haw.) DC.   cholla
Opuntia leptocaulis DC.   desert Christmas cactus
Opuntia phaeacantha Engelm.   prickley pear
Opuntia tunicata (Lehm.) Link & Otto   abrojo
Opuntia violacea Engelm.   purple prickly pear

Chenopodiaceae
Allenrolfea occidentalis (Wats.) O. Ktze.   pickleweed, iodine bush
Atriplex argentea Nutt.   silverscale saltbush
Atriplex canescens (Pursh) Nutt.   four-wing saltbush
Bassia hyssopifolia (Pall.) O. Ktze.   smother-weed
Chenopodium albescens Small   pigweed
Chenopodium album L.   lamb's-quarters
Chenopodium berlandieri Moq.   goosefoot
Cycloloma atriplicifolium (Spreng.) Coult.   winged pigweed
Kochia scoparia (L.) Roth   greenmolly, starwort
Salicornia bigelovii Torr.   samphire
Salicornia utahensis Tidestr.   samphire
Salsoli kali L. (Incl. S. pestifer A. Nels.)   Russian thistle
Suaeda calceoliformis (Hook.) Moq.   broom seepweed
Sueda torreyana Wats.   seepweed

Commelinaceae
Commelina erecta L.   dayflower

Compositae
Ambrosia psilostachya DC.   western ragweed
Aphanostephus ramosissimus DC.   lazy daisy
Artemisia bigelovii Gray   sagebrush
Artemisia dracunculus L. (A. Glauca Pall.)   terragon
Artemisia filifolia Torrey   sand sage
Artemisia ludoviciana Nutt.   mugwort, white sage
Aster ericoides L.   aster
Aster spinosus   Nesom devil-weed
Aster subulatus Michx. including A. exilis Ell. saltmarsh aster
Baccharis pteronioides DC.   yerba de pasmo
Baccharis salicina Torr. & Gray   willow baccharis
Baileya multiradiata Harv. & Gray   desert marigold
Berlandiera lyrata Benth.   green-eyes, chocolate flower
Brickellia californica (Torr. & Gray) Gray   brickelbush
Brickellia grandiflora (Hook.) Nutt.   tassel flower
Brickellia laciniata Gray   cut-leaf brickelbush
Centaurea americana Nutt.   star thistle
(Chrysothamnus (Pall.) Britt.   rabbit-brush
Cirsium ochrocentrum Gray   yellow-spine thistle
Conyza canadensis (L.) Cronq.   horseweed
Conyza coulteri Gray   horseweed

(Crepis ?runciniata (James) T. & G.	hawksbeard
Dicranocarpus parviflora Gray	pitchfork
Dyssodia acerosa	dogweed
Dyssodia pentachaeta (DC.) Robins.	dogweed
Erigeron bellidiastrum Nutt.	western fleabane
Erigeron divergens Torr. & Greene	spreading fleabane
Evax verna Raf. incl. E. multicaulis DC.	rabbit tobacco
Franseria acanthicarpa	ragweed
Gaillardia pinnnatifida Torr.	blanket flower
Gailardia pulchella Foug.	Indian blanket
Grindelia nuda Alph. Wood	gumweed
Gutierrezia microcephala (DC.) Gray	snakeweed
Gutierrezia sarothrae (Pursh) Britt. & Rusby	snakeweed
Gutierrezia sphaerocephala (Gray)	annual snakeweed
Helenium microcephalum DC.)	sneezeweed
Helianthus annuus L.	annual sunflower
Helianthus ciliaris DC.	blueweed
Helianthus paradoxus Heiser	Pecos sunflower
Helianthus petiolaris Nutt.	plains sunflower
Heterotheca latifolia Buckl.	camphor weed
Hymenopappus flavescens Gray	woolly-white
Hymenoxys linearifolia Hook.	annual bitterweed
Hymenoxys odorata DC.	annual bitterweed
Hymenoxys scaposa	bitterweed
Isocoma plurifolia (Torr. & Gray) Greene	jimmy-weed
Iva dealbata Gray	woolly sump-weed
Kuhnia chlorolepis Woot. & Standl.	false boneset
Lactuca serriola L.	prickly lettuce
Leucelene ericoides (Torr.) Greene	baby aster, sand aster
Lygodesmia texana (T. & G.) Greene	skeleton plant
Machaeranthera pinnatifida (Hook.) Shinners	goldenweed
Machaeranthera tanacetifolia (H.B.K.) Nees	Tahoka daisy
Melampodium leucanthum Torr. & Gray	black-foot daisy
Palafoxia sphacelata (Nutt. Ex Torr.) Cory	
Pectis angustifolia Torr.	lemoncillo, lemonweed
Perezia nana	desert holly
Pseudoclappia arenaria Rydb.	
Psilostrophe tangetine (Nutt.) Greene	paper-flower
Ratibida columnifera (Nutt.)	Mexican hat
Ratibida tagetes (James) Barnh.	prairie cone-flower
Sartwellia flaveriae Gray	
Senecio douglasii DC. var. douglasii	threadleaf groundsel
Senecio douglasii DC. var. longilobus	threadleaf groundsel
Senecio riddellii Torr. & Greene	groundsel
Sonchus asper (L.) Hill	sow thistle
Stephanomeria pauciflora (Torr.) A. Nels.	Wire lettuce
Thelesperma megapotamicum (Spreng.) Kuntze	Navajo Tea
Tragopogon dubius Scop.	goat's-beard
Verbesina encelioides (Cav.) Benth. & Hook	crownbeard
Verbesina nana (Gray) Robins.	
Xanthium strumarium L.	cocklebur, abrojo
Zinnia grandiflora Nutt.	desert zinnia

Convolvulaceae
Cressa truxillensis   H.B.K.

Cruciferae
Descurainia pinnata (Walt.) Britt.   tansy mustard
Dithyrea wislizenii Engelm.   spectacle-pod
Draba cuneifolia Nutt. Ex Torr. & Gray   wedgeleaf
Lepidium lasiocarpum Nutt incl. L. wrightii   pepperweed
Lepidium montanum Nutt.   pepperweed
Lesquerella fendleri (Gray) Wats.   bladderpod
Lesquerella gordonii (Gray) Wats.   annual bladderpod
Rorippa sinuata (Nutt.) Hitchc.   yellow-cress
Sisymbrium irio L.   London rocket

Cucurbitaceae
Apodanthera undulata Gray   melon-loco
Cucurbita foetidissima H.B.K.   buffalo-gourd

Cuscutaceae
Cuscuta indecora Chosy   dodder

Cyperaceae
Cyperus esculentus L.   yellow nut-grass
Eleocharis palustris   spikerush
Eleocharis rostellata (Torr.) Torr   spikerush
Scirpus americana Pers.   Olney 3-square, bulrush
Scirpus maritimus L..   alkali bulrush
Scirpus pungens Vahl   common three-square

Eleagnaceae
Eleagnus angustifolia L.   Russian olive

Euphorbiaceae
Argythamnia humilis (Engelm. & Gray)   wild mercury
Croton dioicus Cav.   hierba del gato
Croton pottsii (Kl.) Muell.   leather-weed
Croton texensis (Kl.) Muell.   dove-weed
Euphorbia dentata Michx.   spurge; toothed poinsettia
E. fendleri   fendleri small
E. fendleri   T. & G. var. chaetocalyx (Boiss.) Shinners
E. lata Engelm. in Torr.   Chamaesyce lata (Engelm.) Small
E. micromera Boiss.   Chamaesyce micromera (Boiss.) W. & S.
E. missurica Raf.   Chamaesyce missurica (Raf.) Shinners
E. serpyllifolia Pers.   Chamaesyce serpyllifolia (Pers.) Small
E. serrula Engelm.   Chamaesyce serrula (Engelm.) W. & S.
E. spathulata Lam.   prairie spurge
E. stictospora Engelm.   Chamaesyce stictospora (Eng.) Small

(Fabaceae: see Leguminosae)

(Fumariaceae: see Papaveraceae)

Gentianaceae
Centaurium texense (Griseb.) Fern.   centaury
Eustoma exaltatum (L.) Salisb. ex. G. Don   gentian

Geraniaceae

Erodium texanum Gray	stork's-bill

Gramineae

Andropogon gerardii Vitm.	sensu lato big or sand bluestem
Aristida havardii Vasey = A. barbata Fourn.	Havard three-awn
Aristida purpurea Nutt. var. Fendleriana (Steud.) Vasey	
A. fendleriana Steud.	Fendler's three-awn
Aristida purpurea var. longiseta (Steud.) Vasey	
A. longiseta steud.	red three-awn
Aristida purpurea var. nealleyi (Vasey) Allred	three-awn
A. glauca (Nees) Walp.	
(Aristida purpurea var. purpurea	purple three-awn
Aristida purpurea var. wrightii (Nash) Allred	three-awn
Bothriochloa barbinodis (Lag.) Heter	cane bluestem
Bothriochloa laguroides (DC.) Herter	silver bluestem
Bothriochloa springfieldii (Gould) Parodi	bluestem
Bouteloua barbata Lag.	sixweeks grama
Bouteloua breviseta Vasey	gyp grama
Bouteloua curtipendula (Michx.) Torr.	side-oats grama
Bouteloua eriopoda (Torr.) Torr.	black grama
Bouteloua gracilis	blue grama
Buchloe dactyloides (Nutt.) Engelm.	buffalo grass
Cenchrus incertus M. A. Curtis	sandbur, grassbur
Chloris cucullata Bisch.	hooded windmill grass
Chloris virgata Sw.	feather windmill grass, feather fingergrass
Distlichis spicata (L.) Greene	Saltgrass
Echniochloa muricata (Beauv.) Fern.	cockspur
Elymus canadensis L.	Canada wild-rye
Elymus longifolius (Smith) Gould	squirreltail grass
Elymus smithii (Rydb.) Gould	western wheatgrass
Enneapogon desvauxii Beauv.	spike pappusgrass
Eragrostis barrelieri Daveau	Mediterranean lovegass
Eragrostis cilianensis (All.) Lut. ex Janchen	stinkgrass
Eragrostis curtipedicellata Buckl.	gummy lovegrass
Eragrostis pectinacea (Michx.) Nees ex Steud.	Carolina lovegrass
Erioneuron pilosum (Buckl.) Nash	hairy tridens
Erioneuron pulchellum (Kunth) Tateoka	fluffgrass
Dasyochloa pulchella (Kunth) Steudel	
Hilaria jamesii (Torr.) Benth.	galleta
Hilaria mutica (Buckl.) Benth.	tobosa
Hordeum jubatum L.	foxtail barley
Muhlenbergia arenacea (Buckl.) A.S. Hitchc.	ear muhly
Muhlenbergia arenicola Buckl.	sand muhly
Muhlenbergia asperifolia (Nees & Mey.) Parodi	scratchgrass
Muhlenbergia porteri Scribn.	bush muhly
Muhlenberfia pungens Thurb.	sandhill muhly
(Muhlenbergia repens (Presl) Hitchc.	creeping muhly
Muhlenbergia torreyi (Kunth) Hitch. ex Bush	ringgrass
Munroa squarrosa (Nutt.) Torr.	false buffalo grass
Panicum antidotale Retz	blue panicum
Panicum hallii Vasey	Hall's panicum
Panicum obtusum H.B.K.	vine mesqute
Panicum virgatum L.	switchgrass

Phalaris caroliniana Walt.	canarygrass
Paspalum distichum L.	knotgrass
Phragmites australis (Cav.) Steud.	common reed, carrizo
Polypogon monspeliensis (L.) Desf.	rabbitfoot grass
Polypogon viridis (Gouan)Breistoffer	water bentgrass
Schedonnardus paniculatus (Nutt.) Trel.	tumblegrass
Scleropogon brevifolium Phil.	burrograss
Setaria leucopila (Scribn. & Merr.) K. Schum.	plains bristlegrass
Setaria magna Griseb.	giant foxtail
Sorghum bicolor (L.) Moench = S. vulgare L.	sorghum, milo
Sorghum halepense (L.) Pers.	Johnson grass
Spartina pectinata Link	prairie cordgrass
Sphenopholis obtusata (Michx.) Scribn.	prairie wedgescale
Sporobolus airoides (Torr.) Torr.	alkali sacaton
Sporobolus contractus A.S. Hitchc.	spike dropseed
Sporobolus cryptandrus (Torr.) Gray	sand dropseed
Sporobolus flexuosus (Thurb.) Rydb.	mesa dropseed
Sporobolus giganteus Nash	giant dropseed
Sporobolus nealleyi Vasey	gypgrass
Sporobolus texanus Vasey	Texas dropseed
S. wrightii	Munrogiant sacaton
Tridens albescens (Vasey) W. & S.	white tridens
Tridens muticus (Torr.) Nash	slim tridens
Vulpia octoflora	sixweeks fescue

Hydrophyllaceae

Nama hispidum Gray	purple mat
Phacelia integrifolia Torr.	scorpionweed
Phacelia neomexicana Thurb.	scorpionweed

Juncaceae

Juncus mexicanus	wire rush
Juncus torreyi Cov.	wire rush

Juncaginaceae

Triglochin maritima L.	arrowgrass

Krameriaceae

Krameria lanceolata Torr.	prostrate ratany

Labiatae

Marrubium vulgare L.	horehound
Monarda pectinata Nutt.	plains beebalm, pagoda plant
Salvia reflexa Hornem.	Rocky Mountain sage
Scutellaria drummondii Benth.	skullcap
Teucrium laciniatum Torr.	germander

Leguminosae

Astragalus kentrophyta Gray	
Astragalus lentiginosus Dougl. ex. Hook.	freckled milkvetch
Astragalus mollisimus Torr.	wooly loco
Astragalus nuttalianus DC.	small-flowered milkvetch
Astragalus praelongus Sheldon	stinking milkvetch
Caesalpinia gilliesii (Hook.) Benth.	bird-of-paradise
Caesalpinia jamesii (T. & G.) Fisher	hog potato, rush-pea

Cassia bauhiniodes Gray	two-leaved senna
Cassia roemeriana Scheele	two-leaved senna
Dalea candida Willd.	white prairie clover
Dalea formosa Torr.	Indigo bush; feather plume
Dalea lanata Spreng.	woolly dalea
Gleditsia triacanthos L.	honey locust
Glycyrrhiza lepidota Pursh	wild licorice
Hoffmanseggia glauca (Ortega) Eifert	hog potato, rush-pea
Melilotus albus Desr. ex Lam.	white sweetclover
Mimosa borealis Gray	pink mimosa, fragrant mimosa
Prosopis glandulosa Torr.	mesquite
Robinia neomexicana Gray	locust

Liliaceae

Allium drummondii Regel	wild onion
Asparagus officinalis L.	asparagus
Yucca glauca Nutt.	yucca; Spanish bayonet

Linaceae

Linum aristatum Engelm.	flax
Linum puberulum (Engelm.) Heller	plains flax
Linum rigidum Pursh	flax

Loasaceae

Cevalia sinuata Lag.	
Mentzelia humilis (Gray) J. Darl.	stickleaf
Mentzelia multiflora (Nutt.) Gray	stickleaf
Mentzelia strictissima (W. & S.) J. Darl.	stickleaf

Malvaceae

Malvella leprosa (Ortega) Krapovivkas	alkali mallow
Sphaeralcea angustifolia (Cav.) D. Don	globemallow
Sphaeralcea coccinea (Pursh) Rydb.	globemallow

Moraceae

Morus alba L.	white mulberry

Nyctaginaceae

Abronia fragrans Nutt.	snowballs, sand verbena
Allionia choisya Standl.	umbrellawort, windmills
Allionia incarnata L.	umbrellawort, windmills
Anulocaulis gypsogenus Waterfall	gyp ringstem
Boerhaavia spicata	spiderling
Mirabilis linearis (Pursh) Heimerl.	desert four-o'clock
Selinocarpus diffusus Gray	moonpod
Selinocarpus lanceolatus Woot.	gyp moonpod

Oleaceae

Forestiera neomexicana Gray	New Mexico olive

Onagraceae

Calyophus hartwegii (Benth.) Raven	sundrops
Calyophus tubicula (Gray) Raven	sundrops
Gaura coccinea Pursh	scarlet gaura
Gaura parviflora Hook.	lizard tail, small-flowered gaura

Gaura villosa Torr.   woolly gaura
Oenothera albicaulis Hill   prairie evening primrose
Oenothera caespitosa Nutt.   stemless evening primrose

Orobanchaceae
Orobanche multiflora Nutt.   broomrape

Paperveraceae
Argemone sp. (A. ?squarrosa Grne.)   prickly poppy
Corydalis aurea Willd.   golden smoke

Pedaliaceae
Proboscidea louisianica (Mill.) Thell.   unicorn plant

Plantaginaceae
Plantago patagonica Jacq.   Indian wheat

Plumbaginaceae
Limonium limbatum Small   sea lavender
(Poaceae: see Gramineae)
Polemoniaceae
Eriastrum diffusum (Gray) Mason   wool star
Gilia laxiflora (Coult.) Osterh.   trumpet gilia
Gilia rigidula Benth.   bluebowls

Polygalaceae
Polygala alba Nutt.   milkwort

Polygonaceae
Eriogonum abertianum Torr. in Emory   wild buckwheat
Eriogonum annuum Nutt.   annual buckwheat
Eriogonum jamesii Benth.   wild buckwheat
Eriogonum rotundifolium Benth.   roundleaf buckwheat
Rumex hymenosepalus Torr.   canaigre

Portulacaceae
Portulaca oleracea L.   purslane
Portulaca parvula Gray   purslane
Talinum angustissimum (Gray) W. & S.)   fameflower
Talinum aurantiacum Engelm.   fameflower

Primulaceae
Samolus ebracteactus H.B.K.   water-pimpernel

Ranunculaceae
Delphinium virescens Nutt.   white larkspur, plains larkspur

Rhamnaceae
Condalia lycioides (Gray) Weberb.   lotebush
Microrhamnus ericoides Gray   javelina bush

Rubiaceae
Hedyotis humifusa Gray

Ruppiaceae
Ruppia maritima L.   widgeon-grass

Salicaceae
Populus deltoides H. Marshall   cottonwood

Sapindaceae
Sapindus saponaria L.   soapberry

Saururaceae
Anemopsis californica (Nutt.) Hook. & Arn.   yerba mansa

Scrophulariaceae
Castilleja sessiliflora Pursh   plains paintbrush
Maurandya antirrhinifolia H.&B. Ex. Willd.   snapdragon vine
Penstemon fendleri T. & G.   penstemon

Solanaceae
Chamaesarcha conioides (Moric.) Britt.
Datura quercifolia H.B.K.   thornapple
Datura inoxia Mill.   sacred datura, thornapple
Lycium berlandieri Dunal   wolfberry
Lycium pallidum Miers   pale wolfberry
Nicotiana trigonophylla Dunal   desert tobacco
Physalis lobata Torr.   purple groundcherry
Physalis virginiana Mill.   groundcherry
Solanum eleagnifolium Cav.   horsenettle; nightshade
Solanum rostratum Dunal   Buffalo-bur

Tamaricaceae
Tamarix ramosissima   salt-cedar

Typhaceae
Typha angustifolia L.   cat-tail

Ulmaceae
Celtis reticulata Willd.   hackberry
Ulmus pumila L.   Siberian elm

Umbelliferae
Berula erecta (Huds.) Cov.   water-parsnip
Eurytaenia texana T.&G.   spread-wing
Spermolepis divaricata (DC.) Math. & Const.   scale-seed

Urticaceae
Parietaria floridana Nutt.   pellitory, hammerwort

Verbenaceae
Tetraclea coulteria Gray
Verbena bipinnatifida Nutt.   vervain
Verbena bracteata Lag. & Rodr.   prostrate vervain
Verbena menthaefolia Benth.   mint vervain

Zygophyllaceae

Kallstroemia californica (Wats.) Vail.	carpetweed, caltrop
Kallstroemia grandiflora Gray	desert poppy, caltrop
Kallstroemia parviflora Nort.	carpetweed. caltrop
Larrea tridentata (DC.) Cov.	creosote bush
Tribulus terrestris L.	goathead, puncture vine

Appendix I
Special Status Species of Bitter Lake NWR

Known and Hypothetical, Federal and State Listed Species that Occur at BLNWR. End - endangered, C1 - category 1, C2 - category 2, NME2 - New Mexico endangered group 2, NME1 - New Mexico endangered group 1, PE - proposed listing as endangered.

Status	Common Name	Scientific Name	Occurrence
Mammals			
End	Black-footed ferret	*Mustela nigripes*	hypothetical
C2	Swift fox	*Vulpes velox*	hypothetical
C2	O. little brown bat	*Myotis lucifugus occultus*	wintering
C2	Cave bat	*M. velifer incautus*	wintering
NM2	Least shrew	*Cryptotis parva*	resident
Birds			
End	Am. peregrine falcon	*Falco peregrinus anatum*	migrant
End	Interior least tern	*Sterna antillarum athalaesos*	breeding
End	American bald eagle	*Haliaeetus leucocephalus*	migrant
C2	Baird's sparrow	*Ammodramus bairdi*	migrant
C2	Ferruginous hawk	*Buteo regalis*	wintering
C1	Mountain plover	*Charadrius montanus*	migrant
C2	White-faced ibis	Plegadis chihi	migrant
C2	W. burrowing owl	*Athene cuniculara hypugea*	resident
Reptiles			
C2	Texas horned lizard	*Phrynosoma cornutum*	resident
NM2	River cooter	*Pseudemys concinna*	resident
NM2	W. ribbon snake	*Thamnophis proximus*	resident
Fish			
NM2	Greenthroat darter	*Etheostoma lepidum*	resident
End/NM2	Pecos gambusia	*Gambusia nobilis*	resident
TCH/NM2	Pecos bluntnose shiner	*Notropis simus pecosensis*	resident
C1/NM2	Pecos pupfish	*Cyprinodon pecosensis*	resident
PE/NM1	Ark. River shiner	*Notropis girardi*	resident
C2	Rio Grande shiner	*Notropis jemezanus*	resident
NM2	Mexican tetra	*Astyanax mexicanus*	resident
Aquatic Invertebrates			
NM1	Say's pond snail	*Stagnicola caperata*	resident
C1/NME1	Pecos assiminea snail	*Assiminea pecos*	resident
C1/NME2	Koster's tryonia	*Tryonia kosteri*	resident
C1/NME1	Roswell springsnail	*Pyrgulopsis roswellensis*	resident
C2	Noel's amphipod	*Gammarus desperatus*	resident
Plants			
C1	Pecos sunflower	*Helianthus paradoxus*	resident

Appendix J
Maps

BITTER LAKE NATIONAL WILDLIFE REFUGE
CHAVES COUNTY, NEW MEXICO

UNITED STATES
DEPARTMENT OF THE INTERIOR

UNITED STATES
FISH AND WILDLIFE SERVICE

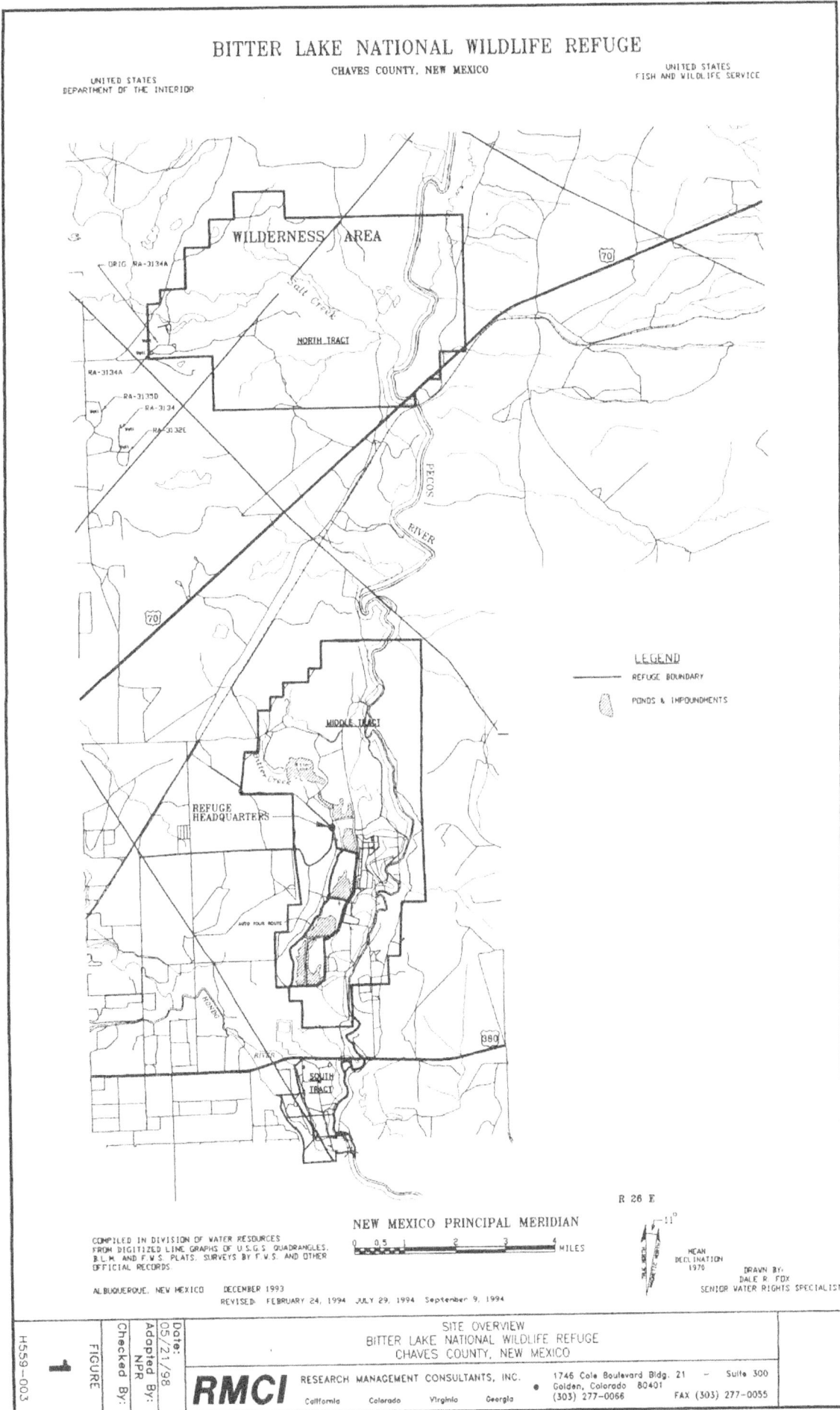

LEGEND

REFUGE BOUNDARY

PONDS & IMPOUNDMENTS

NEW MEXICO PRINCIPAL MERIDIAN

0   0.5   1   2   3   4   MILES

R 26 E

MEAN
DECLINATION
1970

DRAWN BY:
DALE R. FOX
SENIOR WATER RIGHTS SPECIALIST

COMPILED IN DIVISION OF WATER RESOURCES
FROM DIGITIZED LINE GRAPHS OF U.S.G.S. QUADRANGLES,
B.L.M. AND F.W.S. PLATS, SURVEYS BY F.W.S. AND OTHER
OFFICIAL RECORDS.

ALBUQUERQUE, NEW MEXICO   DECEMBER 1993
REVISED: FEBRUARY 24, 1994 JULY 29, 1994 September 9, 1994

SITE OVERVIEW
BITTER LAKE NATIONAL WILDLIFE REFUGE
CHAVES COUNTY, NEW MEXICO

RMCI   RESEARCH MANAGEMENT CONSULTANTS, INC.   1746 Cole Boulevard Bldg. 21   —   Suite 300
Golden, Colorado 80401
California   Colorado   Virginia   Georgia   (303) 277-0066   FAX (303) 277-0055

UNITED STATES
DEPARTMENT OF THE INTERIOR

UNITED STATES
FISH AND WILDLIFE SERVICE

BITTER LAKE NATIONAL WILDLIFE REFUGE
SINKHOLE LOCATIONS
NORTH TRACT and (SALT CREEK WILDERNESS AREA)
CHAVES COUNTY, NEW MEXICO

NEW MEXICO PRINCIPAL MERIDIAN

1 0.5 0 1 MILE

DRAWN BY: DALE R. FOX
SENIOR WATER RIGHTS SPECIALIST

COMPILED IN THE DIVISION OF WATER
RESOURCES FROM U.S.G.S. QUADRANGLES,
F.W.S. PLATS, SURVEYS BY F.W.S. AND
OTHER OFFICIAL RECORDS.

ALBUQUERQUE, NEW MEXICO   FEBRUARY 1995

REVISED: MARCH 1996

GPS SURVEY BY FWS DURING MARCH 20-24, 1995.

SINKHOLE LOCATIONS — NORTH TRACT and SALT CREEK WILDERNESS AREA
BITTER LAKE NATIONAL WILDLIFE REFUGE
CHAVES COUNTY, NEW MEXICO

Date: 05/21/'98

Adopted By: NPR

Checked By:

FIGURE
2

H559-003

RMCI RESEARCH MANAGEMENT CONSULTANTS, INC.
California   Colorado   Virginia   Georgia

1746 Cole Boulevard Bldg. 21 — Suite 300
Golden, Colorado 80401
(303) 277-0066   FAX (303) 277-0055

BITTER LAKE NATIONAL WILDLIFE REFUGE
MIDDLE TRACT
CHAVES COUNTY, NEW MEXICO

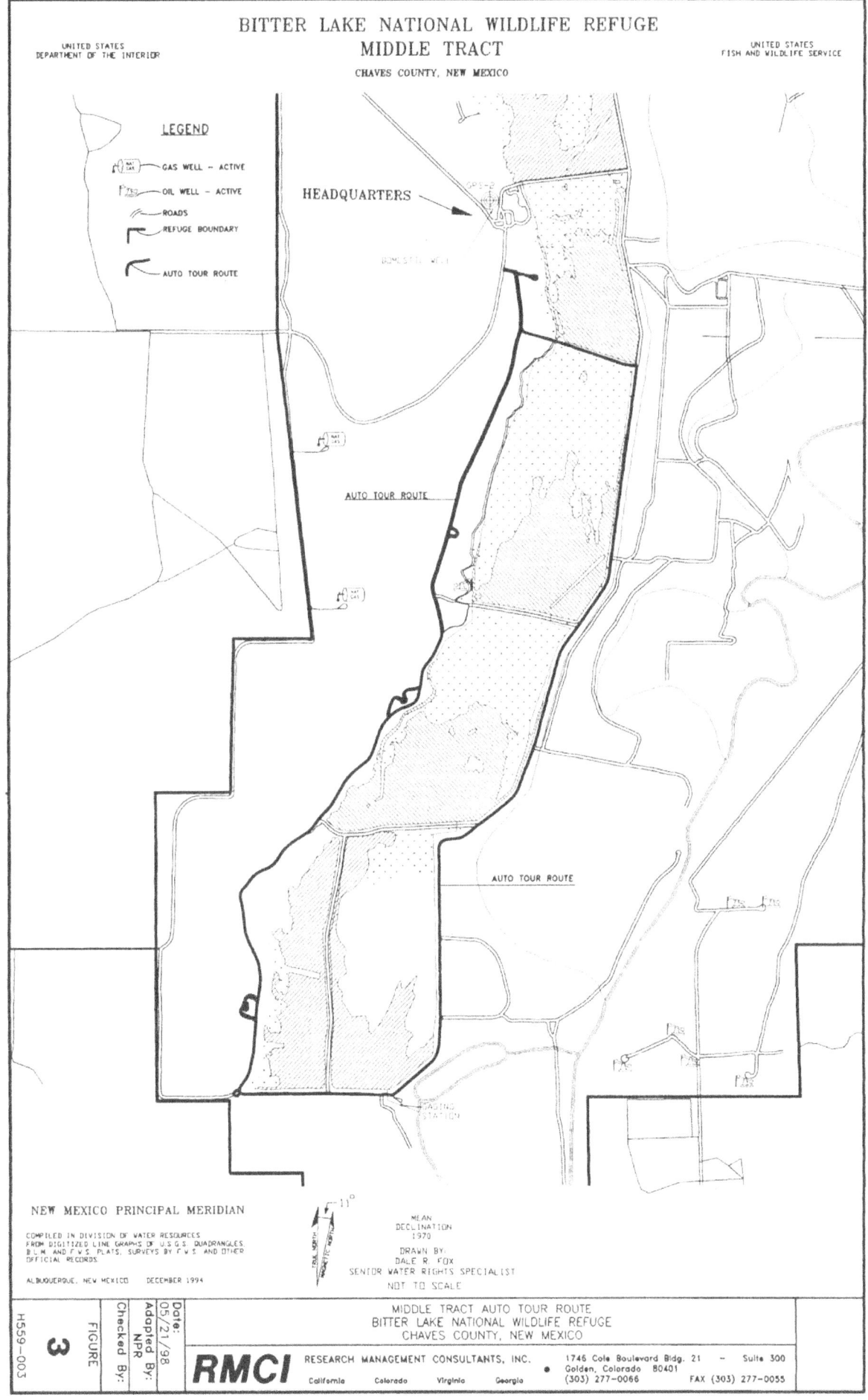

UNITED STATES
DEPARTMENT OF THE INTERIOR

UNITED STATES
FISH AND WILDLIFE SERVICE

LEGEND

- GAS WELL – ACTIVE
- OIL WELL – ACTIVE
- ROADS
- REFUGE BOUNDARY
- AUTO TOUR ROUTE

HEADQUARTERS

AUTO TOUR ROUTE

AUTO TOUR ROUTE

NEW MEXICO PRINCIPAL MERIDIAN

COMPILED IN DIVISION OF WATER RESOURCES
FROM DIGITIZED LINE GRAPHS OF U.S.G.S. QUADRANGLES,
B.L.M. AND F.W.S. PLATS, SURVEYS BY F.W.S. AND OTHER
OFFICIAL RECORDS.

ALBUQUERQUE, NEW MEXICO   DECEMBER 1994

11°

MEAN
DECLINATION
1970

DRAWN BY:
DALE R. FOX
SENIOR WATER RIGHTS SPECIALIST

NOT TO SCALE

MIDDLE TRACT AUTO TOUR ROUTE
BITTER LAKE NATIONAL WILDLIFE REFUGE
CHAVES COUNTY, NEW MEXICO

H559-003

FIGURE 3

Checked By:
Adopted By: NPR
Date: 05/21/98

RMCI RESEARCH MANAGEMENT CONSULTANTS, INC.

California   Colorado   Virginia   Georgia

1746 Cole Boulevard Bldg. 21 — Suite 300
Golden, Colorado 80401
(303) 277-0066   FAX (303) 277-0055

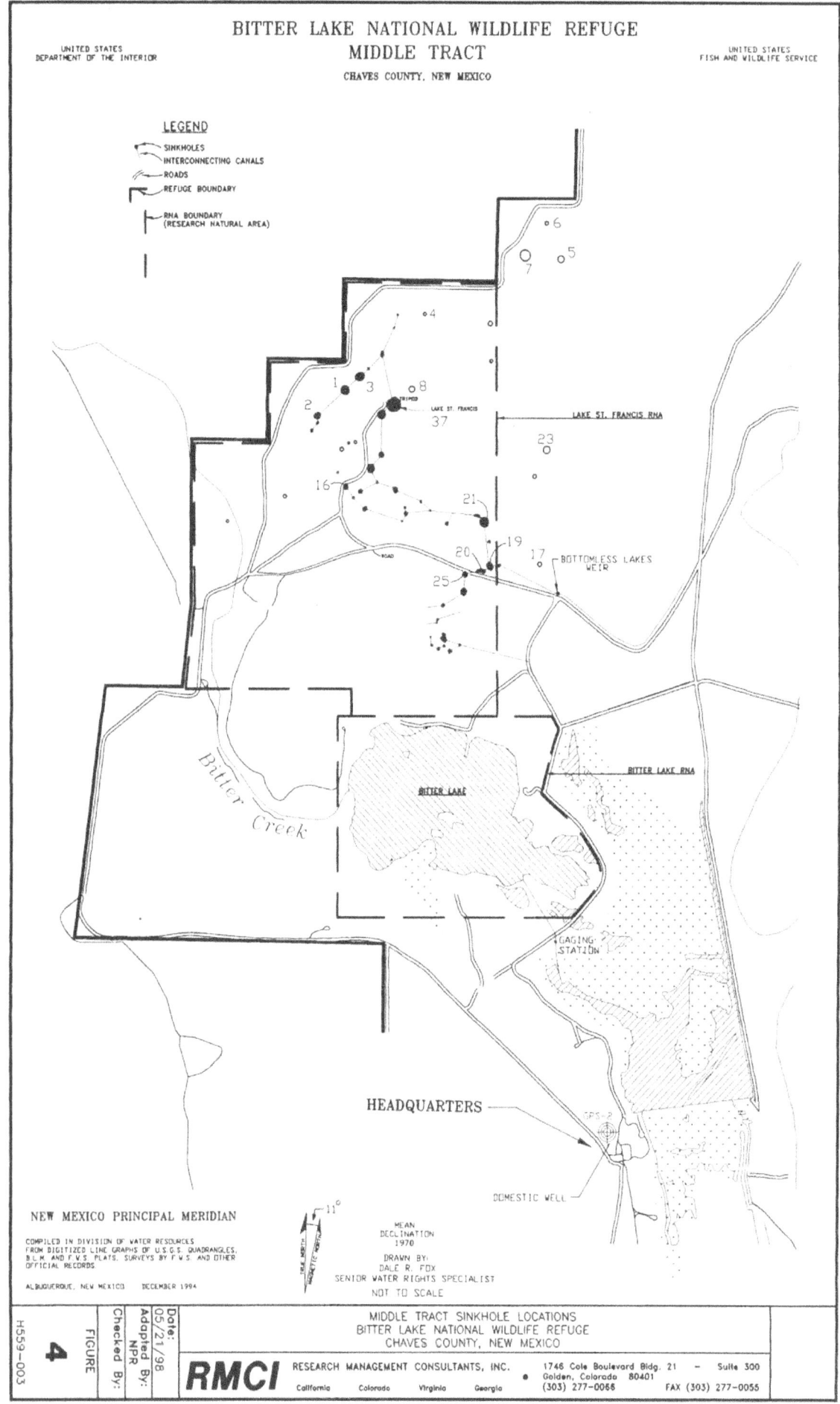

BITTER LAKE NATIONAL WILDLIFE REFUGE
MIDDLE TRACT
CHAVES COUNTY, NEW MEXICO

UNITED STATES
DEPARTMENT OF THE INTERIOR

UNITED STATES
FISH AND WILDLIFE SERVICE

LEGEND
- SINKHOLES
- INTERCONNECTING CANALS
- ROADS
- REFUGE BOUNDARY
- RNA BOUNDARY (RESEARCH NATURAL AREA)

LAKE ST. FRANCIS RNA

LAKE ST. FRANCIS

BOTTOMLESS LAKES WEIR

BITTER LAKE RNA

BITTER LAKE

Bitter Creek

GAGING STATION

HEADQUARTERS

DOMESTIC WELL

NEW MEXICO PRINCIPAL MERIDIAN

COMPILED IN DIVISION OF WATER RESOURCES
FROM DIGITIZED LINE GRAPHS OF U.S.G.S. QUADRANGLES,
B.L.M. AND F.W.S. PLATS, SURVEYS BY F.W.S. AND OTHER
OFFICIAL RECORDS.

ALBUQUERQUE, NEW MEXICO   DECEMBER 1994

11°

MEAN
DECLINATION
1970

DRAWN BY:
DALE R. FOX
SENIOR WATER RIGHTS SPECIALIST

NOT TO SCALE

MIDDLE TRACT SINKHOLE LOCATIONS
BITTER LAKE NATIONAL WILDLIFE REFUGE
CHAVES COUNTY, NEW MEXICO

FIGURE 4

H559-003

Checked By:
Adapted By: NPR
Date: 05/21/98

RMCI RESEARCH MANAGEMENT CONSULTANTS, INC.

California   Colorado   Virginia   Georgia

1746 Cole Boulevard Bldg. 21 — Suite 300
Golden, Colorado 80401
(303) 277-0068   FAX (303) 277-0055

H559\003\CENTRAL   09/24/98

BITTER LAKE NATIONAL WILDLIFE REFUGE
NORTH TRACT and
(SALT CREEK WILDERNESS AREA)
CHAVES COUNTY, NEW MEXICO

UNITED STATES
DEPARTMENT OF THE INTERIOR

UNITED STATES
FISH AND WILDLIFE SERVICE

DIRT ROAD

PIPELINE

SALT CREEK

PECOS RIVER

SANTA FE

AND

TOPEKA

70

COMPILED IN THE DIVISION OF WATER
RESOURCES FROM U.S.G.S. QUADRANGLES,
F.W.S. PLATS, SURVEYS BY F.W.S. AND
OTHER OFFICIAL RECORDS.

ALBUQUERQUE, NEW MEXICO   FEB. 1995

REVISED: MARCH 1995

NEW MEXICO PRINCIPAL MERIDIAN

1   0.5   0   1 MILE

10.5

NEAR
DECLINATION
1982

DRAWN BY:
DALE R. FOX
SENIOR WATER RIGHTS SPECIALIST

GPS SURVEY BY FWS DURING MARCH 20-24, 1995.

| NORTH TRACT and SALT CREEK WILDERNESS AREA
BITTER LAKE NATIONAL WILDLIFE REFUGE
CHAVES COUNTY, NEW MEXICO | Date: 05/21/98 | Check. By: | FIGURE |
| | Adapted By: NPR | | **5** |

RMCI   RESEARCH MANAGEMENT CONSULTANTS, INC.

California   Colorado   Virginia   Georgia

1746 Cole Boulevard Bldg. 21 — Suite 300
Golden, Colorado 80401
(303) 277-0066   FAX (303) 277-0055

H559-003

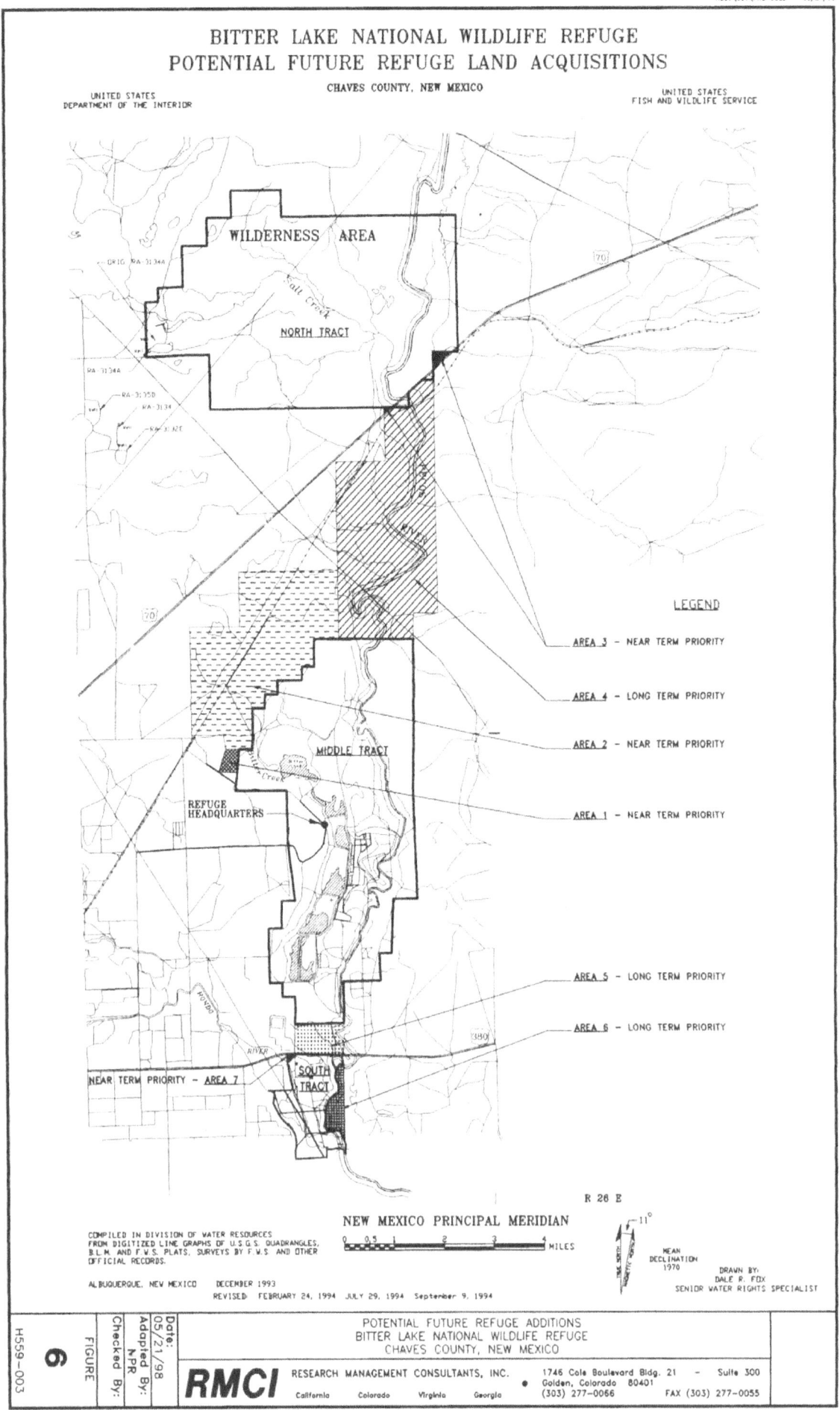

BITTER LAKE NATIONAL WILDLIFE REFUGE
POTENTIAL FUTURE REFUGE LAND ACQUISITIONS
CHAVES COUNTY, NEW MEXICO

UNITED STATES
DEPARTMENT OF THE INTERIOR

UNITED STATES
FISH AND WILDLIFE SERVICE

WILDERNESS AREA

NORTH TRACT

LEGEND

AREA 3 — NEAR TERM PRIORITY

AREA 4 — LONG TERM PRIORITY

AREA 2 — NEAR TERM PRIORITY

AREA 1 — NEAR TERM PRIORITY

MIDDLE TRACT

REFUGE
HEADQUARTERS

AREA 5 — LONG TERM PRIORITY

AREA 6 — LONG TERM PRIORITY

NEAR TERM PRIORITY — AREA 7

SOUTH
TRACT

RIVER

R 26 E

NEW MEXICO PRINCIPAL MERIDIAN

0 0.5 1 2 3 4 MILES

11°

MEAN
DECLINATION
1970

DRAWN BY:
DALE R. FOX
SENIOR WATER RIGHTS SPECIALIST

COMPILED IN DIVISION OF WATER RESOURCES
FROM DIGITIZED LINE GRAPHS OF U.S.G.S. QUADRANGLES,
B.L.M. AND F.W.S. PLATS, SURVEYS BY F.W.S. AND OTHER
OFFICIAL RECORDS.

ALBUQUERQUE, NEW MEXICO   DECEMBER 1993
REVISED: FEBRUARY 24, 1994   JULY 29, 1994   September 9, 1994

POTENTIAL FUTURE REFUGE ADDITIONS
BITTER LAKE NATIONAL WILDLIFE REFUGE
CHAVES COUNTY, NEW MEXICO

RMCI   RESEARCH MANAGEMENT CONSULTANTS, INC.
California   Colorado   Virginia   Georgia

1746 Cole Boulevard Bldg. 21   —   Suite 300
Golden, Colorado   80401
(303) 277-0066   FAX (303) 277-0055

Date: 05/21/98
Adopted By: NPR
Checked By:
FIGURE 6
H559-003

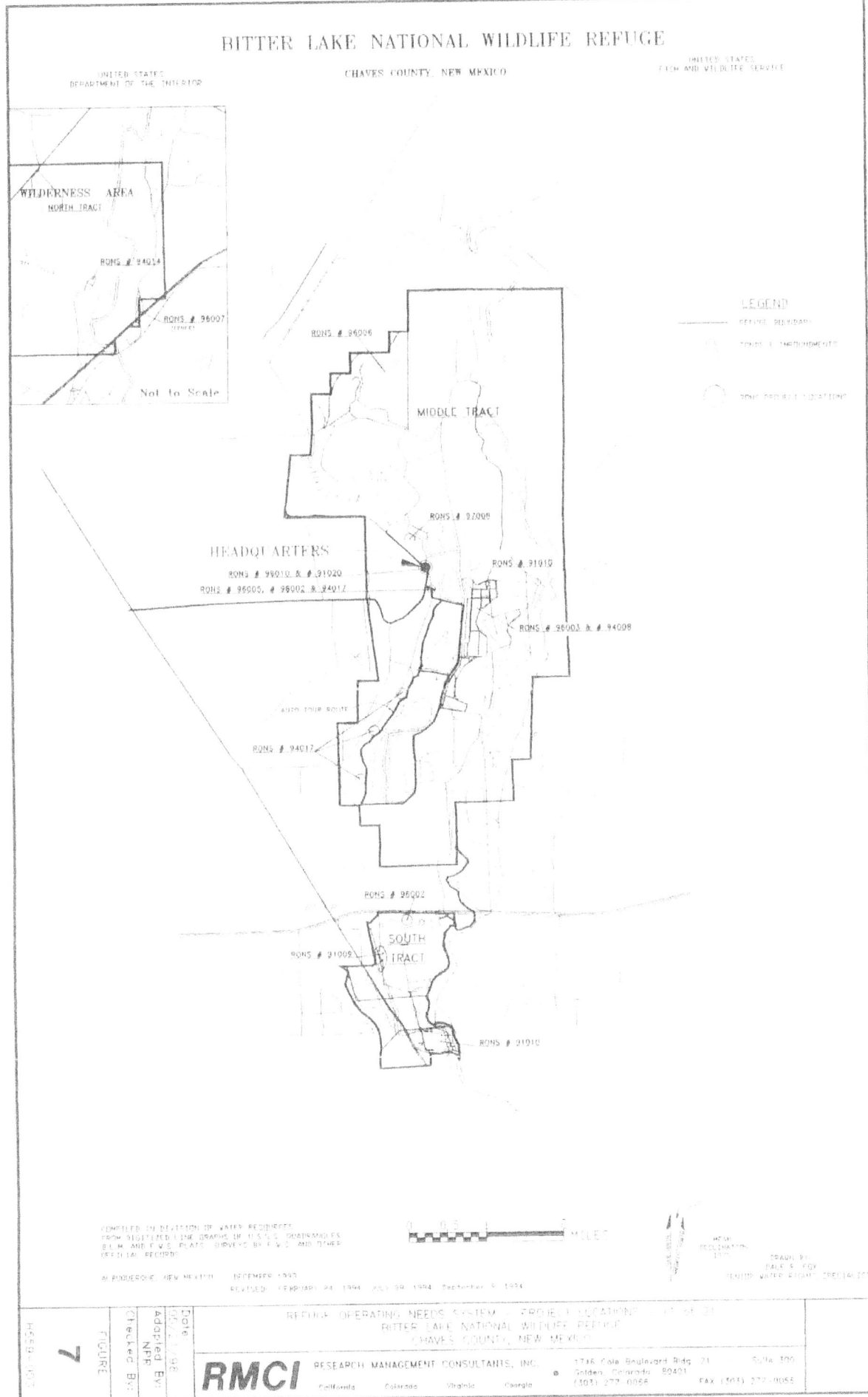

BITTER LAKE NATIONAL WILDLIFE REFUGE

CHAVES COUNTY, NEW MEXICO

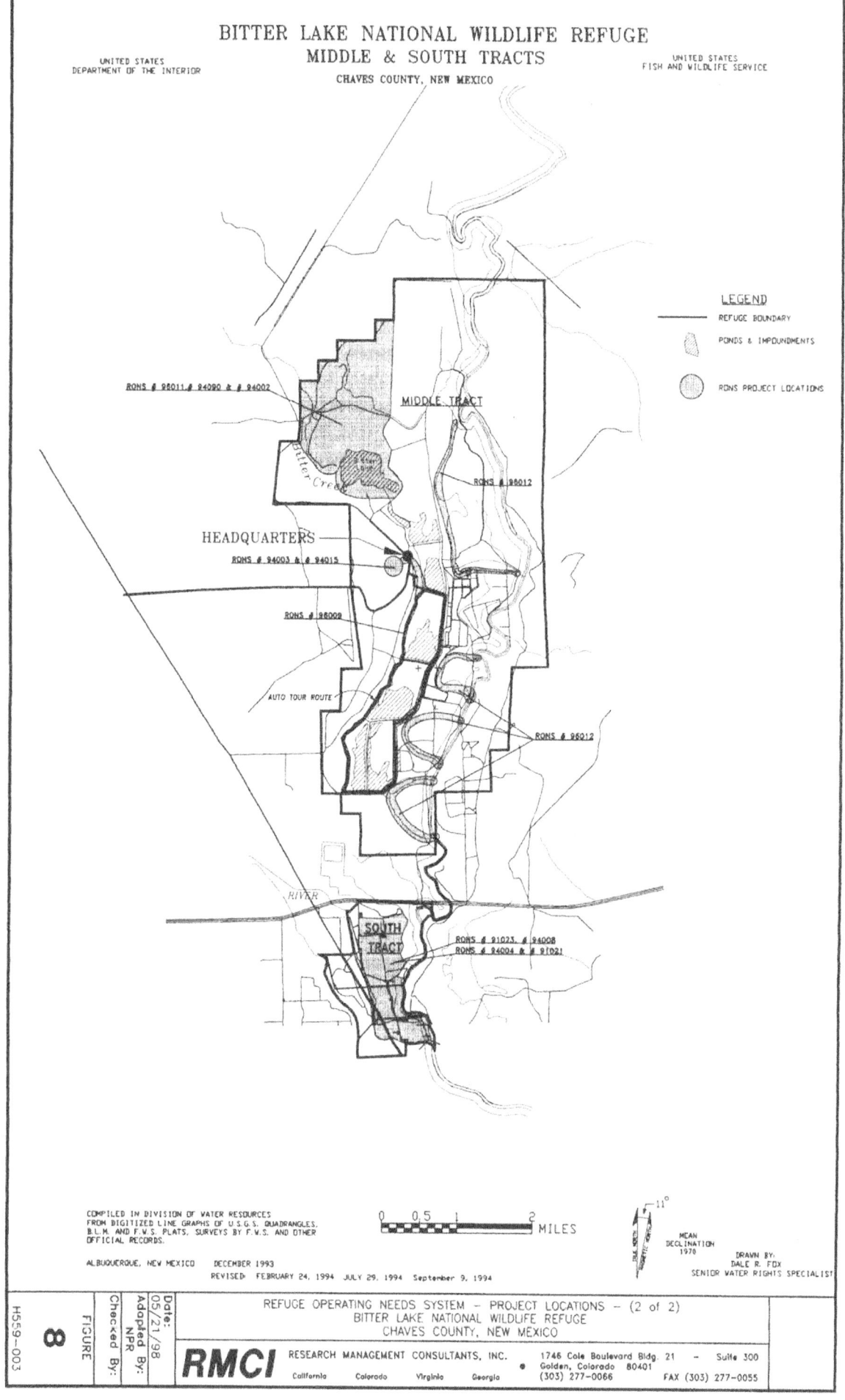

BITTER LAKE NATIONAL WILDLIFE REFUGE
MIDDLE & SOUTH TRACTS
CHAVES COUNTY, NEW MEXICO

UNITED STATES
DEPARTMENT OF THE INTERIOR

UNITED STATES
FISH AND WILDLIFE SERVICE

LEGEND

—————— REFUGE BOUNDARY

PONDS & IMPOUNDMENTS

RONS PROJECT LOCATIONS

RONS # 96011,# 94090 & # 94002

MIDDLE TRACT

RONS # 96012

HEADQUARTERS

RONS # 94003 & # 94015

RONS # 96009

AUTO TOUR ROUTE

RONS # 96012

RIVER

SOUTH TRACT

RONS # 91023, # 94008
RONS # 94004 & # 91021

COMPILED IN DIVISION OF WATER RESOURCES
FROM DIGITIZED LINE GRAPHS OF U.S.G.S. QUADRANGLES,
B.L.M. AND F.W.S. PLATS, SURVEYS BY F.W.S. AND OTHER
OFFICIAL RECORDS.

ALBUQUERQUE, NEW MEXICO   DECEMBER 1993
REVISED: FEBRUARY 24, 1994 JULY 29, 1994 September 9, 1994

0   0.5   1   2
                         MILES

11°

MEAN
DECLINATION
1970

DRAWN BY:
DALE R. FOX
SENIOR WATER RIGHTS SPECIALIST

H559-003

FIGURE

8

Checked By:

Adapted By:
NPR

Date:
05/21/98

REFUGE OPERATING NEEDS SYSTEM – PROJECT LOCATIONS – (2 of 2)
BITTER LAKE NATIONAL WILDLIFE REFUGE
CHAVES COUNTY, NEW MEXICO

RMCI   RESEARCH MANAGEMENT CONSULTANTS, INC.
California   Colorado   Virginia   Georgia

1746 Cole Boulevard Bldg. 21   –   Suite 300
Golden, Colorado 80401
(303) 277-0066   FAX (303) 277-0055

Appendix K
Bitter Lake NWR
Refuge Operating Needs (RONS)

01 | **2) HABITAT RESTORATION: Wetland Restoration: On-Refuge**

1000 acres will be restored ; 1 site(s) will be restored

Portions of the old Pecos River channel, which were isolated through channelization years ago, would be reconnected to the existing river in an effort to provide more natural habitats for threatened fish and other species. The project will require cooperation with hydrologists, fishery biologists, endangered species biologists, and other agencies. Research already conducted has shown that the habitats created by this effort stand to greatly enhance populations of Pecos bluntnose shiners. The project concept is highly supported by both government and non-government cooperators. The Bureau of Reclamation has already begun the planning for this project.

FUNDS ($000) & STAFF NEEDED:

	Construction	Operations	FTEs
First Year:	$250	$3	1.0
Subsequent Years:		$3	0.5

OUTCOMES*:	ES	WF	OMB	HEC	IAF	SDA	RFW	PED	PRC	TOT
	25	0	0	25	0	0	25	25	0	100

PLANNING LINK: ■ Station CMP ■ Station Step-down Mgmt Plan ■ Ecosystem Goal/Plan
■ Station Goal/Objective ■ Recovery Plan ■ Legal Mandate

In addition to refuge specific goals and objectives, Goals #1 and #2 of the Pecos Ecosystem Plan call for restoration and maintenance of systems within the Pecos Watershed that mimic the natural processes capable of supporting diverse plant and animal communities, and to restore and maintain biodiversity. The recovery plan for the federally threatened Pecos bluntnose shiner calls for implementation of habitat restoration techniques.

PROJECT #: ....96012.... RANK - STATION: ...01... DISTRICT: ..999.. REGION: ..999.. NATIONAL: ..999..

---

02 | **8) PUBLIC EDUCATION & RECREATION: Provide Visitor Services**

5,000 additional visitors will visit the station ; 50,000 existing visitors will have new opportunities

The refuge is located in a position to influence a lot of people concerning the value of fish and wildlife conservation. It is important to have a GS-5/7/9 Outdoor Recreation Planner position **reinstated** at Bitter Lake NWR. The position would be used to help build stronger support for the refuge and the Service, to provide high quality educational talks to schools, civic groups, and other organizations in the adjacent community of Roswell (population 50,000), to conduct law enforcement, to adequately plan meaningful interpretive displays on the refuge, and to coordinate a growing volunteer program.

FUNDS ($000) & STAFF NEEDED:

	Construction	Operations	FTEs
First Year:	$0	$40	1.0
Subsequent Years:		$40	1.0

OUTCOMES*:	ES	WF	OMB	HEC	IAF	SDA	RFW	PED	PRC	TOT
	0	0	0	0	0	0	0	50	50	100

PLANNING LINK: ■ Station CMP ■ Station Step-down Mgmt Plan ■ Ecosystem Goal/Plan
■ Station Goal/Objective ☐ Recovery Plan ☐ Legal Mandate

In addition to station goals and Bitter Lake NWR's Public Use Management Plan, The Pecos Ecosystem Plan's Goal #3 has a number of strategies which call for the development, implementation, and maintenance of various public outreach programs and facilities to inform and gain support from the public for management and conservation of Pecos River Ecosystem natural resources.

PROJECT #: ...96008... RANK - STATION: ...02... DISTRICT: ..999.. REGION: ..999.. NATIONAL: ..999..

03 | 1) MONITORING & STUDIES: Studies & Investigations

1 new study(ies) will be conducted ; 10 % of effort will be off-refuge

Comprehensive baseline fish and wildlife inventories are needed to properly and realistically evaluate responses to various resource management techniques. Without this information, educated decisions cannot be made concerning impacts and effects on fish and wildlife under our immediate protection.

FUNDS ($000) & STAFF NEEDED:

	Construction	Operations	FTEs
First Year:	$0	$25	0.5
Subsequent Years:		$25	0.5

OUTCOMES*:	ES	WF	OMB	HEC	IAF	SDA	RFW	PED	PRC	TOT
	20	20	20	20	0	0	20	0	0	100

PLANNING LINK: ■ Station CMP   ■ Station Step-down Mgmt Plan   ■ Ecosystem Goal/Plan
■ Station Goal/Objective   ■ Recovery Plan   ■ Legal Mandate

Every Refuge plan justifies that we know what species occur on the refuge. The Service is mandated to recover numerous listed species on the refuge, and to keep others from becoming listed. Goal #1 of the Pecos Ecosystem Plan identifies a need to restore, protect, and monitor populations designated as endangered, threatened, candidates, or of special concern, and their habitats to a sustainable level.

PROJECT #: 94001   RANK - STATION: 03   DISTRICT: 999   REGION: 999   NATIONAL: 999

---

04 | 1) MONITORING & STUDIES: Studies & Investigations

1 new study(ies) will be conducted ; 0 % of effort will be off-refuge

Although increasingly rare throughout their geographic range, snowy plovers are a fairly common nesting species on the refuge, and utilize the same habitats as endangered interior least terns. Like terns, populations of plovers continue to decline, with limited fledging success by nesting birds. This study would identify habitat parameters important to manage this increasingly rare species.

FUNDS ($000) & STAFF NEEDED:

	Construction	Operations	FTEs
First Year:	$0	$20	0.2
Subsequent Years:		$20	0.2

OUTCOMES*:	ES	WF	OMB	HEC	IAF	SDA	RFW	PED	PRC	TOT
	25	0	50	10	0	0	10	5	0	100

PLANNING LINK: ■ Station CMP   ☐ Station Step-down Mgmt Plan   ■ Ecosystem Goal/Plan
■ Station Goal/Objective   ☐ Recovery Plan   ☐ Legal Mandate

Every Refuge plan justifies that we know what species occur on the refuge. The Service is mandated to recover numerous listed species on the refuge, and to keep others from becoming listed. Goal #1 of the Pecos Ecosystem Plan identifies a need to restore, protect, and monitor populations designated as endangered, threatened, candidates, or of special concern, and their habitats to a sustainable level.

PROJECT #: 94007   RANK - STATION: 04   DISTRICT: 999   REGION: 999   NATIONAL: 999

05 | 2) HABITAT RESTORATION : Upland Restoration: On-Refuge

.250 acres will be restored ; .1 site(s) will be restored

Research Natural Areas on the refuge have become overgrown with exotic saltcedar, threatening unique wetlands and gypsum sinkhole habitats for endangered fish. These areas would be cleared with low impact equipment, such as a "bobcat" which will be purchased and utilized for this specific project. Because of the sensitive nature of the area, private contractors would be avoided, rather, refuge personnel would conduct the work with purchased equipment.

FUNDS ($000) & STAFF NEEDED:		Construction	Operations	FTEs
First Year:		$45	$2	0.5
Subsequent Years:			$2	0.5

OUTCOMES*:	ES	WF	OMB	HEC	IAF	SDA	RFW	PED	PRC	TOT
	20	0	0	20	0	40	20	0	0	100

PLANNING LINK: ■ Station CMP   ■ Station Step-down Mgmt Plan ■ Ecosystem Goal/Plan
■ Station Goal/Objective ☐ Recovery Plan   ☐ Legal Mandate

In addition to refuge specific goals and objectives, Goals #1 and #2 of the Pecos Ecosystem Plan call for restoration and maintenance of systems within the Pecos Watershed that mimic the natural processes capable of supporting diverse plant and animal communities, and to restore and maintain biodiversity.

PROJECT #: ...95011.....   RANK - STATION: ...05...   DISTRICT: ..999..   REGION: ..999..   NATIONAL: ..999..

06 | 6) RESOURCE PROTECTION : Manage Cultural Resources

.1 investigation(s) will be conducted ; .10 site(s) potentially will be documented

While numerous archeological sites exist on the refuge, these sites have not been documented or examined. Sites are scattered throughout upland areas of the refuge, with many (most?) within the Salt Creek Wilderness. Although sites are currently relatively secure from vandalism and "pothunting," some of the sites are in immediate proximity to high public use areas and require immediate evaluation. Before sites can be adequately protected, they must be examined so that detrimental changes can be documented over time. A certified contract archeologist or Service archeologist with refuge staff assistance could perform this initial survey.

FUNDS ($000) & STAFF NEEDED:		Construction	Operations	FTEs
First Year:		$0	$25	0.3
Subsequent Years:			$0	0.0

OUTCOMES*:	ES	WF	OMB	HEC	IAF	SDA	RFW	PED	PRC	TOT
	0	0	0	0	0	35	0	35	30	100

PLANNING LINK: ■ Station CMP   ■ Station Step-down Mgmt Plan ■ Ecosystem Goal/Plan
■ Station Goal/Objective ☐ Recovery Plan   ■ Legal Mandate

In addition to station goals and Bitter Lake NWR's Public Use Management Plan, the Pecos Ecosystem Plan's Goal #3 has a number of streategies which call for the development, implementation, and maintenance of various public outreach programs and facilities to inform and gain support from the public for management and conservation of Pecos River Ecosystem natural resources. Additionally, a federal law, the Archeological Resources Protection Act, calls for attention to this issue.

PROJECT #: ....98001....   RANK - STATION: ...06...   DISTRICT: ..999..   REGION: ..999..   NATIONAL: ..999..

07 | 1) MONITORING & STUDIES: Studies & Investigations

1 new study(ies) will be conducted , 30 % of effort will be off-refuge

The refuge had at least four species of endangered endemic snails, with one of these species apparently extirpated within a year of discovery. Selected wetland habitats on the refuge will be intensively inventoried to determine the continued presence of any of these snail species. Many suitable wetland areas on the refuge have never been surveyed, while others have been checked in an inadequate manner. Management actions on the refuge absolutely depend upon accurate data, and lack of information could lead to extirpation of additional species or populations which are right underneath our control and "protection."

FUNDS ($000) & STAFF NEEDED:

	Construction	Operations	FTEs
First Year:	$0	$5	0.1
Subsequent Years:		$0	0.0

OUTCOMES*:

ES	WF	OMB	HEC	IAF	SDA	RFW	PED	PRC	TOT
50	0	0	25	0	0	25	0	0	100

PLANNING LINK: ■ Station CMP ■ Station Step-down Mgmt Plan ■ Ecosystem Goal/Plan ■ Station Goal/Objective ■ Recovery Plan ■ Legal Mandate

Every Refuge plan justifies that we know what species occur on the refuge. The Service is mandated to recover numerous listed species on the refuge, and to keep others from becoming listed. Goal #1 of the Pecos Ecosystem Plan identifies a need to restore, protect, and monitor populations designated as endangered, threatened, candidates, or of special concern, and their habitats to a sustainable level.

PROJECT #: ...97004....   RANK - STATION: ...07...   DISTRICT: .999..   REGION: ..999..   NATIONAL: ..999..

08 | 2) HABITAT RESTORATION: Wetland Restoration: On-Refuge

100 acres will be restored , 1 site(s) will be restored

During the 1940's, 25 gypsum sinkholes were connected with shallow ditches in an attempt to divert "excess" water to fill impoundments. Since 1955, the water table has dropped to the point where water no longer flows through these ditches, and now is the time to restore this system. Filling the ditches will protect the integrity of individual sinkholes and their representative species composition.

FUNDS ($000) & STAFF NEEDED:

	Construction	Operations	FTEs
First Year:	$0	$35	0.2
Subsequent Years:		$35	0.2

OUTCOMES*:

ES	WF	OMB	HEC	IAF	SDA	RFW	PED	PRC	TOT
20	0	10	20	0	30	20	0	0	100

PLANNING LINK: ■ Station CMP ☐ Station Step-down Mgmt Plan ■ Ecosystem Goal/Plan ■ Station Goal/Objective ■ Recovery Plan ■ Legal Mandate

In addition to refuge specific goals and objectives, Goals #1 and #2 of the Pecos Ecosystem Plan call for restoration and maintenance of systems within the Pecos Watershed that mimic the natural processes capable of supporting diverse plant and animal communities, and to restore and maintain biodiversity.

PROJECT #: ...94020....   RANK - STATION: ...08...   DISTRICT: .999..   REGION: ..999..   NATIONAL: ..999..

09 | 8) PUBLIC EDUCATION & RECREATION: Provide Visitor Services

10,000 additional visitors will visit the station ; 50,000 existing visitors will have new opportunities
The 8-1/2-mile auto tour route is the road used by every single visitor to the refuge, yet this
dirt roadway is rough, viewed with anxiety by some visitors, and needs to be closed during wet
weather. This roadway needs to be reconstructed and upgraded with a gravel surface to provide
safe, all-weather use to allow access for visitors year-round. Work would be done by contract
with refuge oversight and guidance.

FUNDS ($000) & STAFF NEEDED:

	Construction	Operations	FTEs
First Year:	$250	$4	0.5
Subsequent Years:		$4	0.1

OUTCOMES*:

ES	WF	OMB	HEC	IAF	SDA	RFW	PED	PRC	TOT
0	0	0	0	0	0	0	50	50	100

PLANNING LINK: ■ Station CMP   ■ Station Step-down Mgmt Plan ■ Ecosystem Goal/Plan
■ Station Goal/Objective □ Recovery Plan   □ Legal Mandate

In addition to station goals and Bitter Lake NWR's Public Use Management Plan, The Pecos
Ecosystem Plan's Goal #3 has a number of strategies which call for the development,
implementation, and maintenance of various public outreach programs and facilities to inform
and gain support from the public for management and conservation of Pecos River Ecosystem
natural resources.

PROJECT #: ...96009....   **RANK - STATION:** ...09...   **DISTRICT:** ...999...   **REGION:** ..999..   **NATIONAL:** ..999..

---

10 | 6) RESOURCE PROTECTION: Manage Water Rights

(no first measure) ; (no second measure)

As part of a federal reserved water right stipulation requirement expected to be agreed to by
the Service and Department of Justice in late 1996, water levels and surface acres of eight
refuge impoundments must be monitored monthly for a five year period beginning September 1996
and ending August 2001. Failure to conduct this monthly survey will invalidate our federal
reserved water right and could lead to contempt charges.

FUNDS ($000) & STAFF NEEDED:

	Construction	Operations	FTEs
First Year:	$2	$1	0.1
Subsequent Years:		$1	0.1

OUTCOMES*:

ES	WF	OMB	HEC	IAF	SDA	RFW	PED	PRC	TOT
10	20	20	20	0	10	20	0	0	100

PLANNING LINK: ■ Station CMP   ■ Station Step-down Mgmt Plan ■ Ecosystem Goal/Plan
■ Station Goal/Objective ■ Recovery Plan   ■ Legal Mandate

We are mandated by legal stipulation with the state of New Mexico to peform this task.
Furthermore, every pertinent refuge plan requires water monitoring, and every pertinent
threatened or endangered species recovery plan requires habitat monitoring.

PROJECT #: ....97010....   **RANK - STATION:** ...10...   **DISTRICT:** ..999..   **REGION:** ..999..   **NATIONAL:** ..999..

11	6) RESOURCE PROTECTION : Manage Water Rights

.0 (no first measure) ; .0 (no second measure)

This is a study to determine water level changes in sinkholes and Bitter Creek. To document water right needs, relative water levels in seven selected sinkholes in the Lake Saint Francis Research Natural Area need to be measured monthly and related to measured surface flows in Bitter Creek. Failure to conduct this survey could result in loss of federal reserved water rights in the middle tract of the refuge.

FUNDS($000) & STAFF NEEDED:

	Construction	Operations	FTEs
First Year:	$0	$5	0.1
Subsequent Years:		$5	0.1

OUTCOMES*:	ES	WF	OMB	HEC	IAF	SDA	RFW	PED	PRC	TOT
	20	0	0	20	0	20	20	20	0	100

PLANNING LINK: ■ Station CMP   ■ Station Step-down Mgmt Plan ■ Ecosystem Goal/Plan
■ Station Goal/Objective ■ Recovery Plan   ■ Legal Mandate

We are mandated by legal stipulation with the state of New Mexico to peform this task. Furthermore, every pertinent refuge plan requires water monitoring, and every pertinent threatened or endangered species recovery plan requires habitat monitoring.

PROJECT #: __96006__   RANK - STATION: __11__   DISTRICT: __999__   REGION: __999__   NATIONAL: __999__

12	2) HABITAT RESTORATION : Wetland Restoration: On-Refuge

.60 acres will be restored ; 1 site(s) will be restored

Sixty acres of habitat will be developed and managed as "moist soil units" to provide food and habitat for a variety of waterfowl, waterbirds, and other species. The wetland habitat will be restored on old leveled farm fields in the middle tract, where irrigation well water is already assured and protected by state water rights. Managed wetlands are a recognized, efficient, and cost effective method of providing quality habitat for migratory birds.

FUNDS($000) & STAFF NEEDED:

	Construction	Operations	FTEs
First Year:	$40	$5	1.0
Subsequent Years:		$1	0.1

OUTCOMES*:	ES	WF	OMB	HEC	IAF	SDA	RFW	PED	PRC	TOT
	10	30	20	0	0	0	20	10	10	100

PLANNING LINK: ■ Station CMP   ■ Station Step-down Mgmt Plan ■ Ecosystem Goal/Plan
■ Station Goal/Objective □ Recovery Plan   □ Legal Mandate

In addition to refuge specific goals and objectives, Goals #1 and #2 of the Pecos Ecosystem Plan call for restoration and maintenance of systems within the Pecos Watershed that mimic the natural processes capable of supporting diverse plant and animal communities, and to restore and maintain biodiversity.

PROJECT #: __96003__   RANK - STATION: __12__   DISTRICT: __999__   REGION: __999__   NATIONAL: __999__

13 | 8) PUBLIC EDUCATION & RECREATION: Provide Visitor Services

5,000 additional visitors will visit the station ; 50,000 existing visitors will have new opportunities
A new registration building was completed in 1996 at the entrance to the public tour route.
Every single visitor to the refuge passes by this building, which requires one large sign
depicting a map which will also orient visitors to the refuge, inform them of public use
opportunities, and notify them of important regulations.

FUNDS ($000) & STAFF NEEDED:

	Construction	Operations	FTEs
First Year:	$5	$0	0.1
Subsequent Years:		$0	0.0

OUTCOMES*:	ES	WF	OMB	HEC	IAF	SDA	RFW	PED	PRC	TOT
	0	0	0	0	0	20	0	40	40	100

PLANNING LINK: ■ Station CMP   ■ Station Step-down Mgmt Plan   ■ Ecosystem Goal/Plan
■ Station Goal/Objective □ Recovery Plan □ Legal Mandate

In addition to station goals and Bitter Lake NWR's Public Use Management Plan, The Pecos
Ecosystem Plan's Goal #3 has a number of strategies which call for the development,
implementation, and maintenance of various public outreach programs and facilities to inform
and gain support from the public for management and conservation of Pecos River Ecosystem
natural resources.

PROJECT #: __96005__   RANK - STATION: __13__   DISTRICT: __999__   REGION: __999__   NATIONAL: __999__

14 | 8) PUBLIC EDUCATION & RECREATION: Provide Visitor Services

10,000 additional visitors will visit the station ; 50,000 existing visitors will have new opportunities
Two recently completed raised wildlife overlooks require a total of six interpretive signs to
educate the public about biodiversity, native fish management, and habitat management.
Currently, the public comes to the refuge, stands on a nice overlook, and learns nothing
because the Service has yet to provide educational signs. With interpretive signs, the public
could become increasingly aware of the importance of wildlife and fish, our management
programs, and our very mission. Public knowledge and understanding will lead to public
support for our agency and its goals.

FUNDS ($000) & STAFF NEEDED:

	Construction	Operations	FTEs
First Year:	$15	$1	0.1
Subsequent Years:		$0	0.0

OUTCOMES*:	ES	WF	OMB	HEC	IAF	SDA	RFW	PED	PRC	TOT
	20	0	0	20	0	0	20	20	20	100

PLANNING LINK: ■ Station CMP   ■ Station Step-down Mgmt Plan   ■ Ecosystem Goal/Plan
■ Station Goal/Objective ■ Recovery Plan □ Legal Mandate

In addition to station goals and Bitter Lake NWR's Public Use Management Plan, The Pecos
Ecosystem Plan's Goal #3 has a number of strategies which call for the development,
implementation, and maintenance of various public outreach programs and facilities to inform
and gain support from the public for management and conservation of Pecos River Ecosystem
natural resources.

PROJECT #: __96002__   RANK - STATION: __14__   DISTRICT: __999__   REGION: __999__   NATIONAL: __999__

15 | 8) PUBLIC EDUCATION & RECREATION: Provide Visitor Services

5,000 additional visitors will visit the station ; 15,000 existing visitors will have new opportunities
A portion of the 50,000 visitors to the refuge each year stop in at the refuge office, yet
very little information and no display is available to educate them about refuge programs or
the Service mission. To meet this need, an educational exhibit will be installed in the
visitor reception area at refuge headquarters. Four themes; wilderness management, native
fish management, endangered species management, and migratory bird management, will be
portrayed.

FUNDS ($000) & STAFF NEEDED:

			Construction	Operations	PTEs
First Year:			$15	$0	0.2
Subsequent Years:				$0	0.0

OUTCOMES*:	ES	WF	OMB	HEC	IAF	SDA	RFW	PED	PRC	TOT
	0	0	0	0	0	0	0	80	20	100

PLANNING LINK:
■ Station CMP   ■ Station Step-down Mgmt Plan ■ Ecosystem Goal/Plan
■ Station Goal/Objective ■ Recovery Plan   ■ Legal Mandate

In addition to station goals and Bitter Lake NWR's Public Use Management Plan, The Pecos
Ecosystem Plan's Goal #3 has a number of strategies which call for the development,
implementation, and maintenance of various public outreach programs and facilities to inform
and gain support from the public for management and conservation of Pecos River Ecosystem
natural resources.

PROJECT #: ...96010...   RANK - STATION: ...15...   DISTRICT: .999.   REGION: .999.   NATIONAL: .999.

---

16 | 8) PUBLIC EDUCATION & RECREATION: Provide Visitor Services

5,000 additional visitors will visit the station ; 50,000 existing visitors will have new opportunities
A new, up-to-date brochure, listing all vertebrate species that have ever been documented on
the refuge, will be completed and made available to the public. This brochure will be
complete with incorporated original artwork donated by a local artist for the project. Our
current, badly outdated bird list is out of print and out of stock. This is a brochure which
has much demand from the public, and is commonly requested by visitors prior to their visit.
The new brochure would provide a broader base of information for anyone visiting the refuge.

FUNDS ($000) & STAFF NEEDED:

			Construction	Operations	PTEs
First Year:			$0	$8	0.2
Subsequent Years:				$0	0.0

OUTCOMES*:	ES	WF	OMB	HEC	IAF	SDA	RFW	PED	PRC	TOT
	0	0	0	0	0	0	0	50	50	100

PLANNING LINK:
■ Station CMP   ■ Station Step-down Mgmt Plan ■ Ecosystem Goal/Plan
■ Station Goal/Objective □ Recovery Plan   □ Legal Mandate

In addition to station goals and Bitter Lake NWR's Public Use Management Plan, The Pecos
Ecosystem Plan's Goal #3 has a number of strategies which call for the development,
implementation, and maintenance of various public outreach programs and facilities to inform
and gain support from the public for management and conservation of Pecos River Ecosystem
natural resources.

PROJECT #: ...96004...   RANK - STATION: ...16...   DISTRICT: .999.   REGION: .999.   NATIONAL: .999.

17 | 1) MONITORING & STUDIES : Studies & Investigations

1 new study(ies) will be conducted ; 30 % of effort will be off-refuge

A study to determine habitat parameters and densities of rare barking frogs in upland areas of the refuge is needed to help focus upland habitat management projects. The biology of this frog seems closely tied to ground water levels, which may make it an excellent indicator species regarding water conditions including ongoing water right issues and conflicts involving in-stream flow along Bitter Creek. This study would be accomplished by a conrtact biologist with some assistance and direction from refuge personnel.

FUNDS ($000) & STAFF NEEDED:

	Construction	Operations	FTEs
First Year:	$0	$5	0.1
Subsequent Years:		$5	0.1

OUTCOMES*:

ES	WF	OMB	HEC	IAF	SDA	RFW	PED	PRC	TOT
20	0	0	20	0	0	40	20	0	100

PLANNING LINK:
■ Station CMP   □ Station Step-down Mgmt Plan   ■ Ecosystem Goal/Plan
■ Station Goal/Objective   ■ Recovery Plan   ■ Legal Mandate

Every Refuge plan justifies that we know what species occur on the refuge. The Service is mandated to recover numerous listed species on the refuge, and to keep others from becoming listed. Goal #1 of the Pecos Ecosystem Plan identifies a need to restore, protect, and monitor populations designated as endangered, threatened, candidates, or of special concern, and their habitats to a sustainable level.

PROJECT #: ...97002....   RANK - STATION: ....17....   DISTRICT: .999..   REGION: ..999..   NATIONAL: ..999..

---

18 | 3) HABITAT MANAGEMENT : Control Pest Plants

100 acres will be treated ; 2 species will be targeted

Nonnative salt cedar and Russian olive trees continue to invade endangered species critical habitat in Research Natural Areas on the refuge, impacting water tables and native plant and animal communities. Because of sensitive nature of area, intensive handwork is required to chainsaw trees and treat stumps with herbicide. Section-7 consultation has already been approved.

FUNDS ($000) & STAFF NEEDED:

	Construction	Operations	FTEs
First Year:		$30	0.3
Subsequent Years:		$30	0.3

OUTCOMES*:

ES	WF	OMB	HEC	IAF	SDA	RFW	PED	PRC	TOT
30	0	0	30	0	20	20	0	0	100

PLANNING LINK:
■ Station CMP   ■ Station Step-down Mgmt Plan   ■ Ecosystem Goal/Plan
■ Station Goal/Objective   ■ Recovery Plan   ■ Legal Mandate

In addition to refuge specific goals and objectives, and a refuge habitat management plan, Objective #3 of Goal #1 of the Pecos Ecosystem Plan calls for development and support of resource management tactics that emphasize control of non-native plant and animal species to reduce or eliminate negative impacts upon natives species.

PROJECT #: ...94002....   RANK - STATION: ...18..   DISTRICT: .999..   REGION: ..999..   NATIONAL: ..999..

| 19 | 1) MONITORING & STUDIES : Studies & Investigations |

1 new study(ies) will be conducted ; 10 % of effort will be off-refuge

Using pit-fall traps, malaise traps, and other methods, baseline inventory to determine velvet ant species diversity, relative abundance, habitat use, and implications to other refuge resources will be completed with volunteer assistance and contract biologists, with some help and guidance by refuge personnel. There are approximately 30 known species on the refuge, however, the males of many species have not yet been described.

FUNDS ($000) & STAFF NEEDED:

				Construction	Operations	PTEs
First Year:				$0	$5	0.1
Subsequent Years:					$0	0.0

OUTCOMES*:	ES	WF	OMB	HEC	IAF	SDA	RFW	PED	PRC	TOT
	0	0	0	40	0	0	40	20	0	100

PLANNING LINK: ■ Station CMP □ Station Step-down Mgmt Plan ■ Ecosystem Goal/Plan
■ Station Goal/Objective □ Recovery Plan □ Legal Mandate

In addition to refuge specific goals and objectives, Objective 1 of Goal #2 of the Pecos Ecosystem Plan requires restoring, maintaining, and monitoring native communities to meet the needs of native flora and fauna. This includes baseline monitoring of populations of special management interest on selected Service lands.

PROJECT #: __96001__   RANK - STATION: __19__   DISTRICT: __999__   REGION: __999__   NATIONAL: __999__

| 20 | 6) RESOURCE PROTECTION : Law Enforcement |

1 incidents expected to be documented ; 0 citations likely to be issued

To protect native grasslands from abuse and destructive erosion, a one-mile long barbed wire fence will be constructed to a public parking area to limit vehicle access on the east side of the north tract of the refuge. This is an area which has been increasingly abused by off-road traffic, creating additional roadways and damage to uplands. The protection was presented in a refuge compatibility document, which received public comment. The approved project awaits construction.

FUNDS ($000) & STAFF NEEDED:

				Construction	Operations	PTEs
First Year:				$6	$1	0.2
Subsequent Years:					$1	0.1

OUTCOMES*:	ES	WF	OMB	HEC	IAF	SDA	RFW	PED	PRC	TOT
	0	0	0	25	0	0	25	25	25	100

PLANNING LINK: ■ Station CMP ■ Station Step-down Mgmt Plan ■ Ecosystem Goal/Plan
■ Station Goal/Objective □ Recovery Plan ■ Legal Mandate

In addition to other refuge specific goals and objectives, and the 1994 refuge environmental assessment concerning compatible uses, maintaining and restoring biodiversity of terrestrial habitats is called for in Goal #2 of the Pecos Ecosystem Plan.

PROJECT #: __96007__   RANK - STATION: __20__   DISTRICT: __999__   REGION: __999__   NATIONAL: __999__

21 | 1) MONITORING & STUDIES: Studies & Investigations

1 new study(ies) will be conducted ; 50 % of effort will be off-refuge

Baseline information concerning butterfly species present on the refuge, their relative abundance, population dynamics, preferred host plants, and identification of threats will be documented by contract biologists who are experts in this field of study. This work is important toward helping managers make educated decisions regarding the refuge, and will benefit management through a greater understanding of the ecosystem. Without this type of survey, managers will continue to operate and make decisions in the dark.

FUNDS ($000) & STAFF NEEDED:

	Construction	Operations	FTEs
First Year:	$0	$3	0.1
Subsequent Years:		$0	0.0

OUTCOMES*:	ES	WF	OMB	HEC	IAF	SDA	RFW	PED	PRC	TOT
	25	0	0	25	0	0	25	25	0	100

PLANNING LINK: ■ Station CMP   ■ Station Step-down Mgmt Plan ■ Ecosystem Goal/Plan
■ Station Goal/Objective □ Recovery Plan   □ Legal Mandate

In addition to refuge specific goals and objectives, Objective 1 of Goal #2 of the Pecos Ecosystem Plan requires restoring, maintaining, and monitoring native communities to meet the needs of native flora and fauna. This includes baseline monitoring of populations of special management interest on selected Service lands.

PROJECT #: ___97001___   RANK - STATION: ___21___   DISTRICT: __999__   REGION: __999__   NATIONAL: __999__

---

22 | 1) MONITORING & STUDIES: Studies & Investigations

1 new study(ies) will be conducted ; 25 % of effort will be off-refuge

An inventory to determine grasshopper species divesity, relative abundance, seasonal dynamics, and impacts to refuge habitats and trphic levels will be investigated by contract biologists with some refuge assistance and direction. A better understanding of food chains, grassland bird use of habitat, and ecosystem relationships will be the outcome of this study, along with a general baseline set of data.

FUNDS ($000) & STAFF NEEDED:

	Construction	Operations	FTEs
First Year:	$0	$2	0.1
Subsequent Years:		$0	0.0

OUTCOMES*:	ES	WF	OMB	HEC	IAF	SDA	RFW	PED	PRC	TOT
	0	0	20	20	0	0	40	20	0	100

PLANNING LINK: ■ Station CMP   □ Station Step-down Mgmt Plan ■ Ecosystem Goal/Plan
■ Station Goal/Objective □ Recovery Plan   □ Legal Mandate

In addition to refuge specific goals and objectives, Objective 1 of Goal #2 of the Pecos Ecosystem Plan requires restoring, maintaining, and monitoring native communities to meet the needs of native flora and fauna. This includes baseline monitoring of populations of special management interest on selected Service lands.

PROJECT #: ___97003___   RANK - STATION: ___22___   DISTRICT: __999__   REGION: __999__   NATIONAL: __999__

23 | 8) PUBLIC EDUCATION & RECREATION: Outreach

10,000 people will be reached , 400 special event(s) will be hosted

Volunteers and staff will prepare an easy-to-use teacher's guide to assist environmental education outreach into the local school system. Currently there is no such program in any of the schools in the adjacent community of Roswell (population 50,000).

FUNDS ($000) & STAFF NEEDED:

	Construction	Operations	FTEs
First Year:	$0	$3	0.2
Subsequent Years:		$1	0.1

OUTCOMES*:

ES	WF	OMB	HEC	IAF	SDA	RFW	PED	PRC	TOT
0	0	0	0	0	0	0	100	0	100

PLANNING LINK: ■ Station CMP   ■ Station Step-down Mgmt Plan ■ Ecosystem Goal/Plan
■ Station Goal/Objective ☐ Recovery Plan   ☐ Legal Mandate

In addition to station goals and Bitter Lake NWR's Public Use Management Plan, The Pecos Ecosystem Plan's Goal #3 has a number of strategies which call for the development, implementation, and maintenance of various public outreach programs and facilities to inform and gain support from the public for management and conservation of Pecos River Ecosystem natural resources.

PROJECT #: ...97007....   RANK - STATION: ...23....   DISTRICT: ..999..   REGION: ..999..   NATIONAL: ..999..

---

24 | 8) PUBLIC EDUCATION & RECREATION: Provide Visitor Services

additional visitors will visit the station , existing visitors will have new opportunities

Our current brochure is out of print. A revised general refuge brochure is needed for public outreach and education. This new brochure would be designed under the new FWS format and would help meet the local need for refuge information at hotels, the Roswell Chamber of Commerce, and the Public Lands Information Center located at the BLM District Office. A crucial part of the new brochure is a map, an explanation for fish and wildlife conservation, and the purpose of the refuge within the National Wildlife Refuge System.

FUNDS ($000) & STAFF NEEDED:

	Construction	Operations	FTEs
First Year:	$0	$5	0.1
Subsequent Years:		$0	0.0

OUTCOMES*:

ES	WF	OMB	HEC	IAF	SDA	RFW	PED	PRC	TOT
10	10	10	10	0	10	10	20	20	100

PLANNING LINK: ■ Station CMP   ■ Station Step-down Mgmt Plan ■ Ecosystem Goal/Plan
■ Station Goal/Objective ☐ Recovery Plan   ☐ Legal Mandate

In addition to station goals and Bitter Lake NWR's Public Use Management Plan, the Pecos Ecosystem Plan's Goal #3 has a number of strategies which call for the development, implementation, and maintenance of various public outreach programs and facilities to inform and gain support from the public for management and conservation of Pecos River Ecosystem natural resources.

PROJECT #: ....98002....   RANK - STATION: ...24...   DISTRICT: .999.   REGION: ..999..   NATIONAL: ..999..

25 | 8) PUBLIC EDUCATION & RECREATION : Provide Visitor Services

5000 additional visitors will visit the station . 50000 existing visitors will have new opportunities
While this refuge plays a critical role in protecting rare and endangered native fish, the
Service has done a poor job explaining this fact to the public. We need to develop and print
a brochure that specifically identifies the native fish of BLNWR, discussing the status of the
rare species, and informing the public about what the Service is doing to manage rare fish
species on the refuge.

FUNDS($000) & STAFF NEEDED:

	Construction	Operations	FTEs
First Year:	$10	$1	0.1
Subsequent Years:		$1	0.1

OUTCOMES*:	ES	WF	OMB	HEC	IAF	SDA	RFW	PED	PRC	TOT
	25	0	0	25	0	0	25	25	0	100

PLANNING LINK: ▓ Station CMP   ▓ Station Step-down Mgmt Plan   ▓ Ecosystem Goal/Plan
        ▓ Station Goal/Objective ▓ Recovery Plan   ▓ Legal Mandate

In addition to station goals and Bitter Lake NWR's Public Use Management Plan, The Pecos
Ecosystem Plan's Goal #3 has a number of strategies which call for the development,
implementation, and maintenance of various public outreach programs and facilities to inform
and gain support from the public for management and conservation of Pecos River Ecosystem
natural resources.

PROJECT #: ....94013.... RANK - STATION: ...25... DISTRICT: ..999.. REGION: ..999.. NATIONAL: ..999..

26 | 4) FISH & WILDLIFE MANAGEMENT : Predator & Exotic Control

3 species will be targeted . 0 animals will be removed
Salt Creek is located largely within a wilderness area on the north tract of the refuge, and
contains viable isolated populations of Pecos pupfish. We need to build a concrete fish
barrier on salt creek to prevent upstream movement of exotic fish from the Pecos River to
protect populations of native pupfish. This barrier could be designed to be additionally used
to measure surface water flowing into the Pecos River.

FUNDS($000) & STAFF NEEDED:

	Construction	Operations	FTEs
First Year:	$15	$1	0.3
Subsequent Years:		$1	0.1

OUTCOMES*:	ES	WF	OMB	HEC	IAF	SDA	RFW	PED	PRC	TOT
	50	0	0	20	0	10	20	0	0	100

PLANNING LINK: ▓ Station CMP   ▓ Station Step-down Mgmt Plan ▓ Ecosystem Goal/Plan
        ▓ Station Goal/Objective ▓ Recovery Plan   ▓ Legal Mandate

In addition to refuge specific goals and objectives, and a refuge habitat management plan,
Objective #3 of Goal #1 of the Pecos Ecosystem Plan calls for development and support of
resource management tactics that emphasize control of non-native plant and animal species to
reduce or eliminate negative impacts upon natives species.

PROJECT #: ....94014.... RANK - STATION: ...26... DISTRICT: ..999.. REGION: ..999.. NATIONAL: ..999..

27 | 3) HABITAT MANAGEMENT: Farming

100 additional acres will be farmed ; 30 % of effort will be force account

A high water table under refuge farm fields does not benefit maximum farming efficiency. Plastic drain tiles need to be installed in 600 acres of farm fields to allow adequate drainage of fields troubled by hardpan soils and poor perculation of surface water. Problems have led to poor soil aeration, accumulation of salts, and limited productivity.

FUNDS ($000) & STAFF NEEDED:

	Construction	Operations	FTEs
First Year:	$580	$5	0.1
Subsequent Years:		$5	0.1

OUTCOMES*:

ES	WF	OMB	HEC	IAF	SDA	RFW	PED	PRC	TOT
0	40	30	0	0	0	20	10	0	100

PLANNING LINK: ■ Station CMP ■ Station Step-down Mgmt Plan ■ Ecosystem Goal/Plan ■ Station Goal/Objective ☐ Recovery Plan ☐ Legal Mandate

Cropland management is a recognized tool for managing wintering birds and other wildlife, and is justified in the refuge management plan, farming plan, and Pecos Ecosystem Plan.

PROJECT #: ...91023...   RANK - STATION: ...27...   DISTRICT: ...999..   REGION: ...999..   NATIONAL: ...999..

28 | 3) HABITAT MANAGEMENT: Control Pest Plants

1000 acres will be treated ; 1 species will be targeted

Thousands of acres of exotic saltcedar trees are encroaching on native habitats on the refuge, degrading both upland and wetland areas. One operator on a loader can easily and efficiently uproot and pile trees for later burning.

FUNDS ($000) & STAFF NEEDED:

	Construction	Operations	FTEs
First Year:	$100	$23	0.5
Subsequent Years:		$23	0.4

OUTCOMES*:

ES	WF	OMB	HEC	IAF	SDA	RFW	PED	PRC	TOT
20	20	20	20	0	0	20	0	0	100

PLANNING LINK: ■ Station CMP ■ Station Step-down Mgmt Plan ■ Ecosystem Goal/Plan ■ Station Goal/Objective ■ Recovery Plan ■ Legal Mandate

In addition to refuge specific goals and objectives, and a refuge habitat management plan, Objective #3 of Goal #1 of the Pecos Ecosystem Plan calls for development and support of resource management tactics that emphasize control of non-native plant and animal species to reduce or eliminate negative impacts upon natives species.

PROJECT #: ...94005...   RANK - STATION: ...28...   DISTRICT: ...999..   REGION: ...999..   NATIONAL: ...999..

29 | 1) MONITORING & STUDIES: Surveys & Censuses

1 new survey(s) will be conducted ; 0 % of effort will be off-refuge

This survey would sample fish annually using appropriate methods cetermined by habitat type. The information will be used to evaluate changes and trends in fish communities, which would allow managers to initiate necessary management activities.

FUNDS ($000) & STAFF NEEDED:

	Construction	Operations	FTEs
First Year:	$0	$3	0.1
Subsequent Years:		$3	0.1

OUTCOMES*:

ES	WF	OMB	HEC	IAF	SDA	RFW	PED	PRC	TOT
20	0	0	30	0	0	30	20	0	100

PLANNING LINK: ■ Station CMP ☐ Station Step-down Mgmt Plan ■ Ecosystem Goal/Plan ■ Station Goal/Objective ■ Recovery Plan ■ Legal Mandate

Every Refuge plan justifies that we know what species occur on the refuge. The Service is mandated to recover numerous listed species on the refuge, and to keep others from becoming listed. Goal #1 of the Pecos Ecosystem Plan identifies a need to restore, protect, and monitor populations designated as endangered, threatened, candidates, or of special concern, and their habitats to a sustainable level.

PROJECT #: ...94010....   RANK - STATION: ...29....   DISTRICT: ...999..   REGION: ...999..   NATIONAL: ...999..

30 | **3) HABITAT MANAGEMENT : Manage Water Levels**

1200 additional acres will be managed ; 1 new unit(s) will be managed

An excavator is required to conduct continuing restoration and basic management of existing wetland impoundments, marshes, and support canals for optimal management of fish and wildlife populations including several state and federally listed endangered species. Periodic maintenance of ditches, canals, and dikes has been nonexistent since these structures were first constructed in the 1940's.

FUNDS($000) & STAFF NEEDED:

	Construction	Operations	FTEs
First Year:	$125	$5	0.3
Subsequent Years:		$5	0.3

OUTCOMES*:	ES	WF	OMB	HEC	IAF	SDA	RFW	PED	PRC	TOT
	20	20	20	10	0	0	20	0	10	100

PLANNING LINK: ■ Station CMP ■ Station Step-down Mgmt Plan ■ Ecosystem Goal/Plan
■ Station Goal/Objective ■ Recovery Plan ■ Legal Mandate

In addition to refuge specific goals and objectives, Goals #1 and #2 of the Pecos Ecosystem Plan call for restoration and maintenance of systems within the Pecos Watershed that mimic the natural processes capable of supporting diverse plant and animal communities, and to restore and maintain biodiversity.

PROJECT #: 94011 RANK - STATION: 30 DISTRICT: 999 REGION: 999 NATIONAL: 999

---

31 | **3) HABITAT MANAGEMENT : Manage Water Levels**

10,000 additional acres will be managed ; 0 new unit(s) will be managed

There is a tremendous need to purchase a trailer, suitable to haul an existing refuge backhoe, which can be pulled behind our existing dumptruck for efficient use during habitat management projects on the refuge.

FUNDS($000) & STAFF NEEDED:

	Construction	Operations	FTEs
First Year:	$12	$0	0.0
Subsequent Years:		$0	0.0

OUTCOMES*:	ES	WF	OMB	HEC	IAF	SDA	RFW	PED	PRC	TOT
	20	20	20	20	0	0	20	0	0	100

PLANNING LINK: ■ Station CMP ■ Station Step-down Mgmt Plan ■ Ecosystem Goal/Plan
■ Station Goal/Objective ■ Recovery Plan ■ Legal Mandate

In addition to refuge specific goals and objectives, Goals #1 and #2 of the Pecos Ecosystem Plan call for restoration and maintenance of systems within the Pecos Watershed that mimic the natural processes capable of supporting diverse plant and animal communities, and to restore and maintain biodiversity.

PROJECT #: 97005 RANK - STATION: 31 DISTRICT: 999 REGION: 999 NATIONAL: 999

32 | 6) RESOURCE PROTECTION: Wildfire Preparedness

.10. fire(s) expected on-refuge ; .20. fire(s) expected near refuge

With increasing wildfire and prescribed fire responsibilities throughout the state, a contract
to design and construct basic quarters near refuge headquarters is required. This facility
would house a fire crew and equipment to provide 24-hour on-site fire protection by a crew of
six personnel.

FUNDS ($000) & STAFF NEEDED:

		Construction	Operations	FTEs
First Year:		$100	$1	0.5
Subsequent Years:			$2	0.1

OUTCOMES*:	ES	WF	OMB	HEC	IAF	SDA	RFW	PED	PRC	TOT
	10	10	10	20	0	20	20	0	10	100

PLANNING LINK: ■ Station CMP   ■ Station Step-down Mgmt Plan ■ Ecosystem Goal/Plan
■ Station Goal/Objective ☐ Recovery Plan   ☐ Legal Mandate

In addition to refuge specific goals and objectives, Objective 1 of Goal #2 of the Pecos
Ecosystem Plan requires restoring, maintaining, and monitoring native communities to meet the
needs of native flora and fauna. In addition, strategy 1 Of Goal #2 calls for development and
maintenance of a fire program that will achieve resource management objectives on the refuge.

PROJECT #: ...97008...   RANK - STATION: ...32...   DISTRICT: ..999..   REGION: ..999..   NATIONAL: ..999..

33 | 1) MONITORING & STUDIES: Studies & Investigations

.1. new study(ies) will be conducted ; .0. % of effort will be off-refuge

The least shrew is an endangered mammal found in very few locations in the state. Bitter Lake
NWR provides key habitat for the species in New Mexico, yet little is known concerning
distribution, population dynamics, or ecology. This study would determine habitat use,
distribution, and population densities of least shrews on the refuge, but the information
gathered would apply to off-refuge populations in New Mexico.

FUNDS ($000) & STAFF NEEDED:

		Construction	Operations	FTEs
First Year:		$0	$5	0.3
Subsequent Years:			$0	0.0

OUTCOMES*:	ES	WF	OMB	HEC	IAF	SDA	RFW	PED	PRC	TOT
	50	0	0	20	0	0	20	10	0	100

PLANNING LINK: ■ Station CMP   ■ Station Step-down Mgmt Plan ■ Ecosystem Goal/Plan
■ Station Goal/Objective ■ Recovery Plan   ■ Legal Mandate

Every Refuge plan justifies that we know what species occur on the refuge. The Service is
mandated to recover numerous listed species on the refuge, and to keep others from becoming
listed. Goal #1 of the Pecos Ecosystem Plan identifies a need to restore, protect, and monitor
populations designated as endangered, threatened, candidates, or of special concern, and their
habitats to a sustainable level.

PROJECT #: ...97009...   RANK - STATION: ...33...   DISTRICT: ..999..   REGION: ..999..   NATIONAL: ..999..

34 | **8) PUBLIC EDUCATION & RECREATION : Outreach**

20,000 people will be reached ; 900 special event(s) will be hosted

A video will be produced depicting a recent cooperative project to restore refuge wetland habitat. The video will be made available to schools and organizations statewide to increase support and awareness of wetlands and wildlife protection. This project has received the support and potential cost sharing by Ducks Unlimited, Inc.

FUNDS ($000) & STAFF NEEDED:

	Construction	Operations	FTEs
First Year:	$5	$0	0.1
Subsequent Years:		$0	0.1

OUTCOMES*:	ES	WF	OMB	HEC	IAF	SDA	RFW	PED	PRC	TOT
	010	10	10	10	0	0	10	50	0	100

PLANNING LINK: ■ Station CMP   ■ Station Step-down Mgmt Plan ■ Ecosystem Goal/Plan
■ Station Goal/Objective ☐ Recovery Plan   ☐ Legal Mandate

In addition to station goals and Bitter Lake NWR's Public Use Management Plan, The Pecos Ecosystem Plan's Goal #3 has a number of strategies which call for the development, implementation, and maintenance of various public outreach programs and facilities to inform and gain support from the public for management and conservation of Pecos River Ecosystem natural resources.

PROJECT #: 27006   RANK - STATION: 34   DISTRICT: 999   REGION: 999   NATIONAL: 999

---

35 | **8) PUBLIC EDUCATION & RECREATION : Provide Visitor Services**

5000 additional visitors will visit the station ; 50000 existing visitors will have new opportunities

There is a need to develop and erect native fish management interpretive signs, which would identify the native fish on the refuge, discuss the status of rare species, and inform the public about Service management of rare fish on the refuge. The sign would be erected near headquarters at the newly constructed Unit-5 overlook.

FUNDS ($000) & STAFF NEEDED:

	Construction	Operations	FTEs
First Year:	$10	$0	0.1
Subsequent Years:		$0	0.0

OUTCOMES*:	ES	WF	OMB	HEC	IAF	SDA	RFW	PED	PRC	TOT
	25	0	0	25	0	0	25	25	0	100

PLANNING LINK: ■ Station CMP   ■ Station Step-down Mgmt Plan ■ Ecosystem Goal/Plan
■ Station Goal/Objective ■ Recovery Plan   ■ Legal Mandate

In addition to station goals and Bitter Lake NWR's Public Use Management Plan, The Pecos Ecosystem Plan's Goal #3 has a number of strategies which call for the development, implementation, and maintenance of various public outreach programs and facilities to inform and gain support from the public for management and conservation of Pecos River Ecosystem natural resources.

PROJECT #: 94016   RANK - STATION: 35   DISTRICT: 999   REGION: 999   NATIONAL: 999

36	3) HABITAT MANAGEMENT : Farming

100 additional acres will be farmed ; 30 % of effort will be force account

Construct modern facilities to efficiently perform farming and maintenance activities on the refuge. This would include construction of two structures. The first would be a 100' x 50' storage building to protect equipment and vehicles from weather, theft, and vandalism. The second building would include three large bays, floor hoist, storage areas, and restroom facilities. This would allow for the repair of heavy equipment, tractors, farm machinery, and refuge vehicles. Work would be done under contract.

FUNDS ($000) & STAFF NEEDED:

	Construction	Operations	FTEs
First Year:	$290	$40	1.0
Subsequent Years:		$40	1.0

OUTCOMES*:	ES	WF	OMB	HEC	IAF	SDA	RFW	PED	PRC	TOT
	0	40	30	0	0	0	20	10	0	100

PLANNING LINK: ■ Station CMP   ■ Station Step-down Mgmt Plan ■ Ecosystem Goal/Plan
■ Station Goal/Objective □ Recovery Plan   □ Legal Mandate

Farming is a cost effective management tool used to maintain concentrated populations of wintering birds and other wildlife. The Refuge CMP, farming plan, and Pecos River Ecosystem Plan each justify this activity.

PROJECT #: ....91009....   RANK - STATION: ...36....   DISTRICT: .999.   REGION: .999.   NATIONAL: .999.

37	2) HABITAT RESTORATION : Upland Restoration: On-Refuge

10 acres will be restored ; 1 site(s) will be restored

Ten acres of upland habitat near headquarters will be planted with native overstory vegetation. Irrigation will be provided by trenching a line to the site from existing domentic well. Managed riparian habitat will provide important stopover and breeding habitat for neotropical birds.

FUNDS ($000) & STAFF NEEDED:

	Construction	Operations	FTEs
First Year:	$10	$1	0.1
Subsequent Years:		$1	0.1

OUTCOMES*:	ES	WF	OMB	HEC	IAF	SDA	RFW	PED	PRC	TOT
	0	0	60	0	0	0	20	0	20	100

PLANNING LINK: □ Station CMP   □ Station Step-down Mgmt Plan ■ Ecosystem Goal/Plan
■ Station Goal/Objective □ Recovery Plan   □ Legal Mandate

In addition to refuge specific goals and objectives, Goals #1 and #2 of the Pecos Ecosystem Plan call for restoration and maintenance of systems within the Pecos Watershed that mimic the natural processes capable of supporting diverse plant and animal communities, and to restore and maintain biodiversity.

PROJECT #: ...91003....   RANK - STATION: ...37...   DISTRICT: .999.   REGION: .999.   NATIONAL: .999.

| 38 | 8) PUBLIC EDUCATION & RECREATION: Provide Visitor Services |

5000 additional visitors will visit the station ; 50000 existing visitors will have new opportunities following establishment of native vegetation (RONS project 94003), a foot trail will be designated and developed to provide wildlife oriented recreation, such as birding, in a "controlled" setting near headquarters to minimize disturbance to wildlife. Developed hiking trails on the refuge are currently nearly nonexistent, yet there is increasing public demand for this type of activity. Without designated trails, visitors will be tempted to enter sensitive or closed refuge areas.

FUNDS ($000) & STAFF NEEDED:

		Construction	Operations	FTEs
First Year:		$10	$1	0.2
Subsequent Years:			$1	0.1

OUTCOMES*:	ES	WF	OMB	HEC	IAF	SDA	RFW	PED	PRC	TOT
	0	0	0	0	0	0	0	50	50	100

PLANNING LINK: ▣ Station CMP   ▣ Station Step-down Mgmt Plan ▣ Ecosystem Goal/Plan
▣ Station Goal/Objective ☐ Recovery Plan   ☐ Legal Mandate

In addition to station goals and Bitter Lake NWR's Public Use Management Plan, The Pecos Ecosystem Plan's Goal #3 has a number of strategies which call for the development, implementation, and maintenance of various public outreach programs and facilities to inform and gain support from the public for management and conservation of Pecos River Ecosystem natural resources.

PROJECT #: ...94015....   RANK - STATION: ...38...   DISTRICT: ...999...   REGION: ...999...   NATIONAL: ...999...

| 39 | 8) PUBLIC EDUCATION & RECREATION: Provide Visitor Services |

5000 additional visitors will visit the station ; 50000 existing visitors will have new opportunities We need to design and install up to four shade ramadas using natural rock or brick facing to provide a screened view of wildlife utilizing refuge ponds. Existing obtrusive metal structures will be removed from overlook sites. Bitter lake is in a desert grassland community, where the sun shines 300 days each year. It can be very hot during the summer, and visitors do not stay too long outside of their vehicles. Shaded overlooks would permit increased numbers of visitors to stay and learn more about the refuge.

FUNDS ($000) & STAFF NEEDED:

		Construction	Operations	FTEs
First Year:		$40	$0	0.4
Subsequent Years:			$0	0.0

OUTCOMES*:	ES	WF	OMB	HEC	IAF	SDA	RFW	PED	PRC	TOT
	0	0	0	0	0	0	0	50	50	100

PLANNING LINK: ▣ Station CMP   ▣ Station Step-down Mgmt Plan ▣ Ecosystem Goal/Plan
▣ Station Goal/Objective ☐ Recovery Plan   ☐ Legal Mandate

In addition to station goals and Bitter Lake NWR's Public Use Management Plan, The Pecos Ecosystem Plan's Goal #3 has a number of strategies which call for the development, implementation, and maintenance of various public outreach programs and facilities to inform and gain support from the public for management and conservation of Pecos River Ecosystem natural resources.

PROJECT #: ...94017....   RANK - STATION: ...39...   DISTRICT: ...999...   REGION: ...999...   NATIONAL: ...999...

40 | 2) HABITAT RESTORATION : Upland Restoration: On-Refuge

140 acres will be restored , 1 site(s) will be restored

Approximately 140 acres of abandoned farm fields require reseeding with native alkali sacaton grass. Fields are too salty for crop production and should be managed as native grasslands.

FUNDS ($000) & STAFF NEEDED:

	Construction	Operations	FTEs
First Year:	$0	$45	0.1
Subsequent Years:		$0	0.0

OUTCOMES*:	ES	WF	OMB	HEC	IAF	SDA	RFW	PED	PRC	TOT
	0	0	50	25	0	0	20	5	0	100

PLANNING LINK: ■ Station CMP   □ Station Step-down Mgmt Plan ■ Ecosystem Goal/Plan
■ Station Goal/Objective □ Recovery Plan   □ Legal Mandate

In addition to refuge specific goals and objectives, Goals #1 and #2 of the Pecos Ecosystem Plan call for restoration and maintenance of systems within the Pecos Watershed that mimic the natural processes capable of supporting diverse plant and animal communities, and to restore and maintain biodiversity.

PROJECT #: ...94008....   RANK - STATION: ...40...   DISTRICT: ...999..   REGION: ...999..   NATIONAL: ...999..

41 | 3) HABITAT MANAGEMENT : Control Pest Plants

10 acres will be treated , 1 species will be targeted

A 10.2-acre field on the south tract farm has become overgrown with noxious johnsongrass, greatly impacting productivity. The field will be taken out of production for one year and repeatedly treated with herbicide to remove persistent johnsongrass.

FUNDS ($000) & STAFF NEEDED:

	Construction	Operations	FTEs
First Year:	$0	$5	0.1
Subsequent Years:		$0	0.0

OUTCOMES*:	ES	WF	OMB	HEC	IAF	SDA	RFW	PED	PRC	TOT
	0	40	30	20	0	0	10	0	0	100

PLANNING LINK: ■ Station CMP   ■ Station Step-down Mgmt Plan ■ Ecosystem Goal/Plan
■ Station Goal/Objective □ Recovery Plan   □ Legal Mandate

In addition to refuge specific goals and objectives, and a refuge habitat management plan, Objective #3 of Goal #1 of the Pecos Ecosystem Plan calls for development and support of resource management tactics that emphasize control of non-native plant and animal species to reduce or eliminate negative impacts upon natives species.

PROJECT #: ...94004....   RANK - STATION: ...41...   DISTRICT: ...999..   REGION: ...999..   NATIONAL: ...999..

42 | 3) HABITAT MANAGEMENT : Farming

100 additional acres will be farmed , 25 % of effort will be force account

There is a need to drill an additional irrigation well on the south tract to increase the supply of quality water for refuge crops and moist soil units. The project would include drilling a 200 foot deep well, and would include casing, pump, and electrical hookup.

FUNDS ($000) & STAFF NEEDED:

	Construction	Operations	FTEs
First Year:	$35	$1	0.1
Subsequent Years:		$1	0.1

OUTCOMES*:	ES	WF	OMB	HEC	IAF	SDA	RFW	PED	PRC	TOT
	0	40	30	10	0	0	20	0	0	100

PLANNING LINK: ■ Station CMP   ■ Station Step-down Mgmt Plan ■ Ecosystem Goal/Plan
■ Station Goal/Objective □ Recovery Plan   □ Legal Mandate

Intensive farming is a reconized management tool for accomplishing wintering bird population objectives identified in the refuge CMP, farming plan, and Pecos River Ecosystem Plan.

PROJECT #: ...91021....   RANK - STATION: ...42...   DISTRICT: ...999..   REGION: ...999..   NATIONAL: ...999..

43 | 8) PUBLIC EDUCATION & RECREATION: Provide Visitor Services

5000 additional visitors will visit the station ; 50,000 existing visitors will have new opportunities
There is a critical need to build a public restroom facility beside the refuge headquarters
that is especially designed to accomodate handicapped visitors.

FUNDS ($000) & STAFF NEEDED:

		Construction	Operations	FTEs
First Year:		$45	$1	0.1
Subsequent Years:			$1	0.1

OUTCOMES*:	ES	WF	OMB	HEC	IAF	SDA	RFW	PED	PRC	TOT
	0	0	0	0	0	0	0	50	50	100

PLANNING LINK: ■ Station CMP   ■ Station Step-down Mgmt Plan ■ Ecosystem Goal/Plan
                ■ Station Goal/Objective □ Recovery Plan   ■ Legal Mandate

This refuge is open to the public and receives an average of 50,000 visitors each year. We
have a goal to accomodate the public with basic facilities including a restroom. We have a
legal mandate to accomodate handicapped visitors.

PROJECT #: ....21020....   RANK - STATION: ...43...   DISTRICT: ..999.   REGION: ..999..   NATIONAL: ..999..

---

44 | 2) HABITAT RESTORATION: Upland Restoration: On-Refuge

65 acres will be restored ; 1 site(s) will be restored
The Pecos River has changed its course, causing extreme bank erosion. If left unchecked, a 65
acre farm field and an irrigation well will be lost and washed away. A Corps permit and
assistance would be sought for erosion control, perhaps rip-rap. Work would be contracted.

FUNDS ($000) & STAFF NEEDED:

		Construction	Operations	FTEs
First Year:		$200	$25	0.5
Subsequent Years:			$0	0.0

OUTCOMES*:	ES	WF	OMB	HEC	IAF	SDA	RFW	PED	PRC	TOT
	0	40	30	10	0	0	20	0	0	100

PLANNING LINK: ■ Station CMP   ■ Station Step-down Mgmt Plan ■ Ecosystem Goal/Plan
                ■ Station Goal/Objective □ Recovery Plan   □ Legal Mandate

Intensive farming is a recognized method of managing large numbers of wintering waterfowl and
other wildlife. A multitude of plans identify this need to manage croplands, which stand to
be lost through unchecked erosion.

PROJECT #: ....91010....   RANK - STATION: ...44...   DISTRICT: ..999.   REGION: ..999..   NATIONAL: ..999..

MONITORING & STUDIES : Studies & Investigations

MEASURES: 1 studies will be conducted; 25 % of effort will be off-refuge

An inventory to determine Aquatic invertebrate species divesity, relative abundance, seasonal dynamics, and impacts to refuge habitats and trophic leveles will be investigated by contract biologists with some refuge assistance and direction. A better understanding of food chains, and ecosystem relationships will be the outcome of this study, along with a general baseline set of data.

ADDITIONAL FUNDS NEEDED ($000):	One-Time	Recurring Base	First Year Need
Construction Costs............................			
Operations: Personnel Costs..................	5		
Equipment Cost...................	1		
Facility Cost...................			
Services/Supplies...............			
Miscellaneous Costs.............			
TOTAL Operations Cost......................	6		6

ADDITIONAL PERMANENT STAFF NEEDED:	FTEs	Cost ($000)
Managers.....................................		$0
Biologists..................................		$0
Resource Specialists.......................		$0
Education/Recreation Staff.................		$0
Law Enforcement............................		$0
Clerical/Administrative....................		$0
Maintenance/Equipment Operation.............		$0
TOTAL FTEs Needed.....................		$0

EMPHASIS: % Critical health & safety; 100% Critical resource protection; % Critical mission; % Other important needs

OUTCOMES*:	ES	WF	OMB	HEC	IAF	SDA	RW	PED	FAR	PRC	TOT
		25	25	25					25		100

PLANNING LINKS: Station Goal/Objective; FWS Ecosystem Goal/Plan; Station CCP/equivalent pre-10/97

In addition to refuge specific goals and objectives, Objective 1 of Goal #2 of the Pecos Ecosystem Plan requires restoring, maintaining, and monitoring native communities to meet the needs of native flora and fauna. This includes baseline monitoring of populations of special management interest on selected Service lands.

PROJECT #: ....98100.... RANK - STATION: ..999.. DISTRICT: REGION: NATIONAL:

MEASURES: 1 studies will be conducted

It is suspected that the formation of the gypsum sinkholes and associated wetlands on Bitter Lake NWR occurred during the very early Pleistocene, with some occurring in their present state since the Cretaceous Period. This would be a long enough time for speciation in isolated Odonata, and initial collecting has determined that as many as 17 species never before collected in New Mexico may occur on the refuge. It is suspected that at least a portion of these species have never been described and are new to science. Research is needed to collect, identify, and document the distribution of these important endemic wetland indicator species.

ADDITIONAL FUNDS NEEDED ($000):	One-Time	Recurring Base	First Year Need
Construction Costs...........................			
Operations: Personnel Costs.................	6		
Equipment Cost..................			
Facility Cost...................			
Services/Supplies...............			
Miscellaneous Costs.............	1		
TOTAL Operations Cost.......................	7		7

ADDITIONAL PERMANENT STAFF NEEDED:	FTEs	Cost ($000)
Managers...................................		$0
Biologists.................................		$0
Resource Specialists.......................		$0
Education/Recreation Staff.................		$0
Law Enforcement............................		$0
Clerical/Administrative....................		$0
Maintenance/Equipment Operation............		$0
TOTAL FTEs Needed......................		$0

EMPHASIS: 0% Critical health & safety; 75% Critical resource protection; 25% Critical mission; 0% Other important needs

OUTCOMES*:	ES	WF	OMB	HEC	IAF	SDA	RW	PED	FAR	PRC	TOT
	50			25					25		100

PLANNING LINKS: Station CCP approved 10/97+; Station Goal/Objective; FWS Recovery Plan; Legal Mandate; FWS Ecosystem Goal/Plan

Every Refuge plan justifies that we know what species occur on the refuge. The Service is mandated to recover numerous listed species on the refuge, and to keep others from becoming listed. Goal #1 of the Pecos Ecosystem Plan identifies a need to resore, protect, and monitor populations designated as endangered, threatened, candidates, or of special concern, and their habitats to a sustainable level.

PROJECT #: ...99.001.... RANK - STATION: .999. DISTRICT: .999. REGION: .999. NATIONAL: .999.

MEASURES: 1 wildlife surveys will be conducted

A draft Conservation Agreement, crucial to the continued survival of the Pecos pupfish, identifies the need to secure refuge habitats to protect this rare species. While a life history research project for the pupfish is currently underway, and an adequate fish barrier is under construction at the South Weir on the refuge, it is extremely important to begin initiating an annual monitoring program each late summer/early fall in up to 5 selected refuge impoundments to check for invasion by sheepshead minnows, which are displacing native Pecos pupfish in other localities. This effort is crucial to recovery and protection of the Pecos pupfish.

ADDITIONAL FUNDS NEEDED ($000):	One-Time	Recurring Base	First Year Need
Construction Costs...........................			
Operations: Personnel Costs.................		4	
Equipment Cost...................			
Facility Cost...................			
Services/Supplies...............	1		
Miscellaneous Costs.............			
TOTAL Operations Cost......................	1	4	5

ADDITIONAL PERMANENT STAFF NEEDED:	FTEs	Cost ($000)
Managers...................................		$0
Biologists.................................	0.1	$4
Resource Specialists.......................		$0
Education/Recreation Staff.................		$0
Law Enforcement............................		$0
Clerical/Administrative....................		$0
Maintenance/Equipment Operation............		$0
TOTAL FTEs Needed......................	0.1	$4

EMPHASIS: 0% Critical health & safety; 100% Critical resource protection; 0% Critical mission; 0% Other important needs

OUTCOMES*:	ES	WF	OMB	HEC	IAF	SDA	RW	PED	FAR	PRC	TOT
	50								50		100

PLANNING LINKS: Station CCP approved 10/97+; Station Goal/Objective; Station Step-down Mgmt Plan; FWS Recovery Plan; FWS Ecosystem Goal/Plan; Other Major Plan; Legal Mandate

Every Refuge plan justifies that we know what species occur on the refuge. The Service is mandated to recover numerous listed species on the refuge, and to keep others from becoming listed. Goal #1 of the Pecos Ecosystem Plan identifies a need to resore, protect, and monitor populations designated as endangered, threatened, candidates, or of special concern, and their habitats to a sustainable level.

PROJECT #: ....99002.... RANK - STATION: .999. DISTRICT: .999. REGION: .999. NATIONAL: .999.

Refuge Management Information System - Refuge Operating Needs System   Needs Printout #3
Bitter Lake NWR - 9/14/98 - Page 47   - 9/14/98 -

Page 47

MEASURES: 1 studies will be conducted

Noel's amphipod is endemic to Bitter Lake NWR and occurs nowhere else in the world, having been extirpated from two other adjacent locations since its discovery. Amphipods are extremely sensitive to water quality, and are excellent indicators of contaminants and other factors. While the species appears secure on the refuge, little is known about its basic ecology (reproductive period, predation, activity periods, key habitat parameters, etc). This investigation would provide important answers to questions relating to refuge habitat management practices and has indirect implications in protecting endangered fish species as well.

ADDITIONAL FUNDS NEEDED ($000):

	One-Time	Recurring Base	First Year Need
Construction Costs.............................			
Operations: Personnel Costs...................	15		
Equipment Cost....................			
Facility Cost.....................			
Services/Supplies................	1		
Miscellaneous Costs..............			
TOTAL Operations Cost.........................	16		16

ADDITIONAL PERMANENT STAFF NEEDED:

	FTEs	Cost ($000)
Managers.....................................		$0
Biologists...................................		$0
Resource Specialists.........................		$0
Education/Recreation Staff...................		$0
Law Enforcement..............................		$0
Clerical/Administrative......................		$0
Maintenance/Equipment Operation.............		$0
TOTAL FTEs Needed......................		$0

EMPHASIS: 0% Critical health & safety; 100% Critical resource protection; 0% Critical mission; 0% Other important needs

OUTCOMES*:	ES	WF	OMB	HEC	IAF	SDA	RW	PED	FAR	PRC	TOT
	50			25					25		100

PLANNING LINKS: Station CCP approved 10/97+; Station Goal/Objective; FWS Recovery Plan; FWS Ecosystem Goal/Plan; Legal Mandate; Other Major Plan

Every Refuge plan justifies that we know what species occur on the refuge. The Service is mandated to recover numerous listed species on the refuge, and to keep others from becoming listed. Goal #1 of the Pecos Ecosystem Plan identifies a need to resore, protect, and monitor populations designated as endangered, threatened, candidates, or of special concern, and their habitats to a sustainable level.

PROJECT #: ....99003.... RANK - STATION: .999. DISTRICT: .999. REGION: .999. NATIONAL: .999.

Refuge Management Information System - Refuge Operating Needs System   Needs Printout #1
Bitter Lake NWR - 9/14/98 - Page 48   - 9/14/98 -

Page 48

MEASURES: ; 1 habitat surveys will be conducted
___

Fire effects short term and long term monitoring are needed to properly and realistically evaluate responses to the use of fire as a resource managment tool on vegetative species and communities. Without this information, informed decisions cannot be made concerning impacts and effects on the vegetative resources under our immediate protection.

ADDITIONAL FUNDS NEEDED ($000):	One-Time	Recurring Base	First Year Need
Construction Costs............................			
Operations: Personnel Costs..................		27	
Equipment Cost...................	3		
Facility Cost...................			
Services/Supplies...............			
Miscellaneous Costs.............			
TOTAL Operations Cost.......................	3	27	30

ADDITIONAL PERMANENT STAFF NEEDED:	FTEs	Cost ($000)
Managers.....................................		$0
Biologists..................................	0.9	$27
Resource Specialists.......................		$0
Education/Recreation Staff.................		$0
Law Enforcement............................		$0
Clerical/Administrative....................		$0
Maintenance/Equipment Operation............		$0
TOTAL FTEs Needed......................	0.9	$27

EMPHASIS: 0% Critical health & safety; 100% Critical resource protection; 0% Critical mission; 0% Other important needs

OUTCOMES*:	ES	WF	OMB	HEC	IAF	SDA	RW	PED	FAR	PRC	TOT
	10	10	10	20		10	10	10	10	10	100

PLANNING LINKS: Station CCP approved 10/97+; Station Goal/Objective; Station Step-down Mgmt Plan; FWS Recovery Plan; FWS Ecosystem Goal/Plan; Other Major Plan; Legal Mandate
___

All of the above refuge planning documents as well as the Fire Management Plan concur with the need for comprehensive baseline data for species, vegetative communities, and habitats. Goal #1 of the Pecos Ecosystem Plan identifies a need to monitor habitat.
___

PROJECT #: ...99004....   RANK - STATION: ..999..   DISTRICT: ..999..   REGION: ..999..   NATIONAL: ..999..

Refuge Management Information System - Refuge Operating Needs System
Bitter Lake NWR - 9/14/98 - Page 49   - 9/14/98 -   Needs Printout #3

Page 49

999 PLANNING & ADMINISTRATION : General Administration

Due to the relatively isolated location of the refuge, and the fact that headquarters and three government quarters are at the "end of the line" concerning utility distribution, it is a common event to lose power during inclement weather events (high winds, thunderstorms, snow). The facility was without power for four days straight at subzero temperatures during December 1997. Two back-up generators should be installed to provide essential electrical power, heating, cooling, telephone, radio communication, and meet administrative needs. One generator would supply the Headquarters and the other would supply the three quarters.

ADDITIONAL FUNDS NEEDED ($000):	One-Time	Recurring Base	First Year Need
Construction Costs..........................			
Operations: Personnel Costs.................			
Equipment Cost...................	20		
Facility Cost....................			
Services/Supplies...............			
Miscellaneous Costs.............			
TOTAL Operations Cost.......................	.20		20

ADDITIONAL PERMANENT STAFF NEEDED:	FTEs	Cost ($000)
Managers...................................		$0
Biologists.................................		$0
Resource Specialists.......................		$0
Education/Recreation Staff..................		$0
Law Enforcement............................		$0
Clerical/Administrative....................		$0
Maintenance/Equipment Operation.............		$0
TOTAL FTEs Needed......................		$0

EMPHASIS: 50% Critical health & safety; 0% Critical resource protection; 25% Critical mission; 25% Other important needs

OUTCOMES*:	ES	WF	OMB	HEC	IAF	SDA	RW	PED	FAR	PRC	TOT
	10	10	10	20		10	10	10	10	10	100

PLANNING LINKS: Station CCP approved 10/97+; Station Goal/Objective; FWS Ecosystem Goal/Plan; Other Major Plan; Legal Mandate

In addition to station goals and the Bitter Lake NWR Draft Comprehensive Conservation Plan, the pecos Ecosystem Plan's Goal #3 has a number of strategies which call for the development, implementation, and maintenance of of facilites which support public use management on the refuge.

PROJECT #: ....99005....   RANK - STATION: ..999..   DISTRICT: ..999..   REGION: ..999..   NATIONAL: ..999..

Refuge Management Information System - Refuge Operating Needs System   Needs Printout #3
Bitter Lake NWR - 9/14/98 - Page 50   - 9/14/98 -

Page 50

MEASURES: 3000 refuge acres will be restored

About 7,000 acres of Bitter Lake NWR has been invaded by exotic salt cedar trees, damaging wetlands and impacting native grasslands. Current techniques in large tracts of salt cedar utilizing bulldozers and prescribed fire has been cost effective, but current equipment cannot remove the tree's root crown, which resprouts after disturbance. Acquisition of a root plow and root rake which would be pulled behind existing heavy equipment will effectively kill salt cedar. Through this method, at least 3,000-acres of exotic vegetation can be permanently removed and restored to native conditions at low cost.

ADDITIONAL FUNDS NEEDED ($000):	One-Time	Recurring Base	First Year Need
Construction Costs............................			
Operations: Personnel Costs..................			
Equipment Cost...................	20		
Facility Cost...................			
Services/Supplies...............			
Miscellaneous Costs.............			
TOTAL Operations Cost.......................	20		20

ADDITIONAL PERMANENT STAFF NEEDED:	FTEs	Cost ($000)
Managers....................................		$0
Biologists.................................		$0
Resource Specialists........................		$0
Education/Recreation Staff..................		$0
Law Enforcement.............................		$0
Clerical/Administrative.....................		$0
Maintenance/Equipment Operation.............		$0
TOTAL FTEs Needed.....................		$0

EMPHASIS: 0% Critical health & safety; 100% Critical resource protection; 0% Critical mission; 0% Other important needs

OUTCOMES*:	ES	WF	OMB	HEC	IAF	SDA	RW	PED	FAR	PRC	TOT
	10	10	10	20		10	10	10	10	10	100

PLANNING LINKS: Station CCP approved 10/97+; Station Goal/Objective; Station Step-down Mgmt Plan; FWS Recovery Plan; FWS Ecosystem Goal/Plan; Other Major Plan; Legal Mandate

In addition to refuge specific goals and objectives, Goals #1 and #2 of the Pecos Ecosystem Plan call for restoration and maintenance of systems within the Pecos Watershed that mimic the natural processes capable of supporting diverse plant and animal communities, and to restore and maintain biodiversity.

PROJECT #: 99006   RANK - STATION: 999   DISTRICT: 999   REGION: 999   NATIONAL: 999

Appendix L
Proposed Full Staffing

Future staffing needs presented in the following list and chart reflects currently allocated positions throughout the planning period including title changes, proposed increases in grade level and conversions from part time to full time permanent positions.

Proposed Full Staffing Level:

Project Leader-GS-0485-13 PFT
Refuge Operations Specialist-GS-0485-9/11/12 PFT
Fire Management Officer-GS-0401-12 PFT
Assistant Fire Management Officer-GS-401-7/9 PFT
Prescribed Fire Specialist-GS-0401-7/9 PFT
Fish & Wildlife Biologist-GS-0486/0401-7/9/11 PFT
Outdoor Recreation Specialist-GS-023-7/9/11 PFT
Fish and Wildlife Biologist-GS-0486/0401-7/9 PFT
Engineering Equipment Operator-WG-5716-10 PFT
Maintenance Worker-WG-4749-10 PFT
Maintenance Worker-WG-4749-08 PFT
Laborer-WG-3502-3 TFT
Administrative Support Assistant-GS-0303-6/7 PFT
Office Automation Clerk-GS-0326-4/5 PFT
Fire Program Assistant-GS-0455-5 PFT
Range Technician (Engine Boss)-GS-0455-5/6 PFT
Firefighter-GS-0455-4/5 TFT
Firefighter-GS-0455-4/5 TFT
Firefighter-GS-0455-4/5 TFT
Prescribed Fire Monitor Crew Leader-GS-0404-4/5 PFT
Prescribed Fire Monitor-GS-0404-4 TFT
Prescribed Fire Monitor-GS-0404-4 TFT
YCC Group Leader GS-0186-05 TFT

Bold denotes positions not currently authorized.

Proposed Full Staffing Level
Bitter Lake NWR

bolded box denotes positions not currently authorized

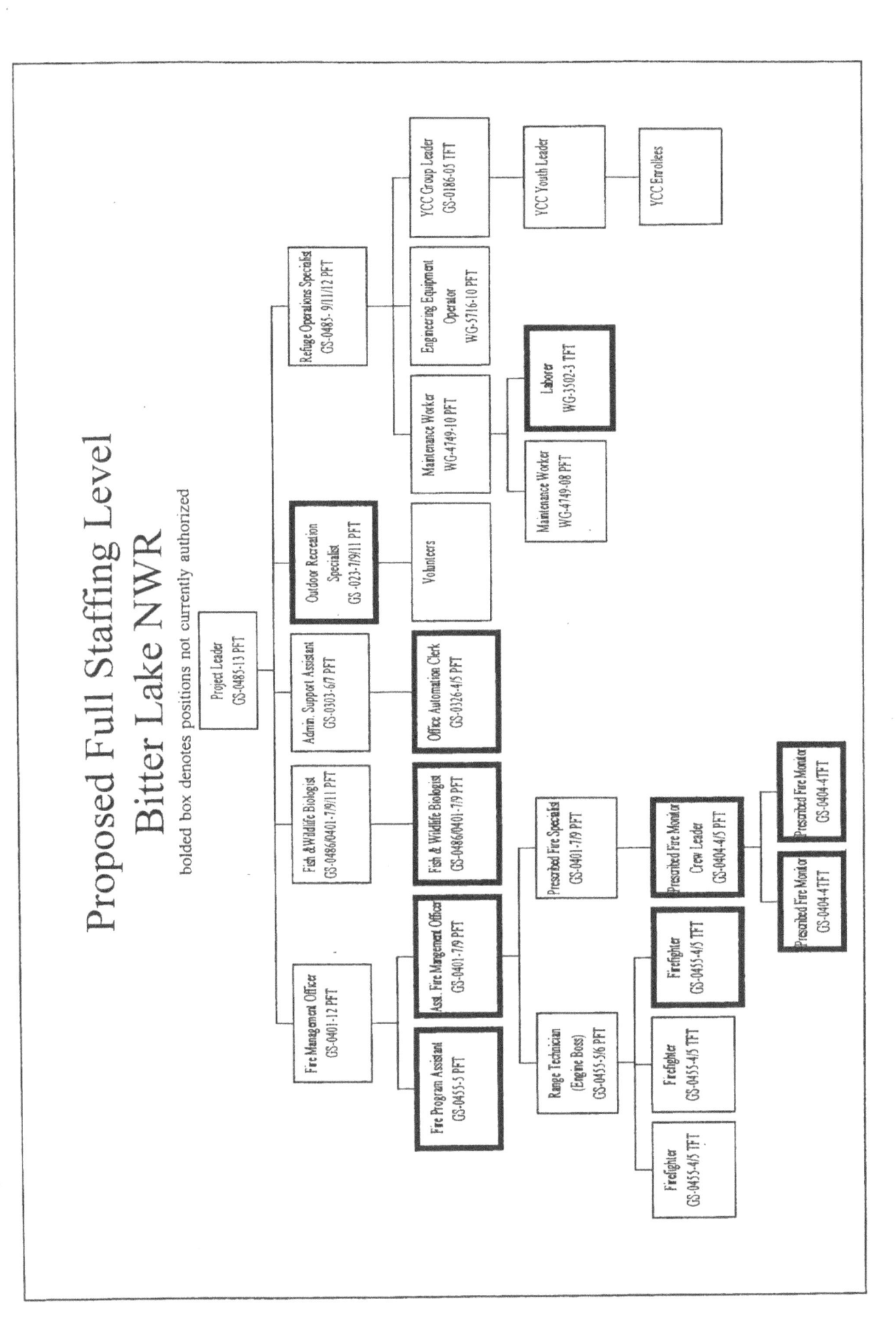

U.S. FISH AND WILDLIFE SERVICE
ENVIRONMENTAL ACTION MEMORANDUM

Within the spirit and intent of the Council on Environmental Quality's regulations for implementing the National Environmental Policy Act (NEPA) and other statutes, orders, and policies that protect fish and wildlife resources, I have established the following administrative record and have determined that the action of approval of the proposals reflected in the Bitter Lake National Wildlife Refuge Comprehensive Conservation Plan and in the proposed management framework alternative in the attached Environmental Assessment:

_____   is a categorical exclusion as provided by 516 DM 6 Appendix 1 section B(4). No further documentation will be made.

___X___   is found not to have significant environmental effects as determined by the attached Environmental Assessment and Finding of No Significant Impact.

_____   is found to have special environmental conditions as described in the attached Environmental Assessment. The attached Finding of No Significant Impact will not be final nor any actions taken pending a 30 day period for public review (40 CFR 1501.4(e)(2)).

_____   is found to have significant effects, and therefore a "notice of Intent" will be published in the Federal Register to prepare an Environmental Impact Statement before the project is considered further.

_____   is denied because of environmental damage, Service policy, or mandate.

_____   is an emergency situation. Only those actions necessary to control the immediate impacts of the emergency will be taken. Other related actions remain subject to NEPA review.

Other supporting documents: **Finding of No Significant Impact, Bitter Lake NWR Comprehensive Conservation Plan and Environmental Assessment**

_____ _____
Director/Regional Director   Date

(1)_____ 9/24/98
Initiator   Date

(2)_____ 9/24/98
Geographic ARD AZ/ NM   Date

(3)_____ 9/25/98
NEPA Coordinator/ Region 2   Date

Finding of No Significant Impact

Comprehensive Conservation Plan and Environmental Assessment
for Bitter Lake National Wildlife Refuge

The U.S. Fish and Wildlife Service has developed a Comprehensive Conservation Plan (CCP) and Environmental Assessment (EA) for the Bitter Lake National Wildlife Refuge. Through a program of consultation and public involvement, the Service has outlined the various problems and opportunities (i.e., issues) confronting the refuge. The CCP and EA outlines these issues and how the Service intends to address them over the next 10 to 20 years.

Approval of this CCP constitutes the definition of appropriate management approaches and establishment of refuge goals, objectives and strategies leading to the achievement of the refuge's purposes and mission of the National Wildlife Refuge System. The CCP formalizes six goals which will result in: (1) Restoration, enhancement, and protection of biological diversity, land, wildlife and habitat; (2) Restoration of hydrological resources and improvements to water quality; (3) Provision of compatible recreational uses; (4) Protection of cultural resources; (5) Strengthening and maintenance of effective relationships with other governmental agencies and stakeholders; (6) Improvements to refuge staffing and funding. Some of the specific changes to the existing program changes include but are not necessarily limited to the following strategies:

- A restoration of 250 acres of Research Natural Areas and 1000 acres in other areas by removal and control of non-native salt cedar;
- Restoration of over story vegetation near the refuge headquarters (10 acres) and providing appropriate irrigation;
- Restoration of 140 acres of abandoned agricultural fields as grasslands;
- Enhance promotion of environmental education in area schools and organizations on the value of short grass prairie ecosystems;
- Acquire identified land parcels as appropriate as they become available on a willing seller basis;
- Restoration of 100 acres of habitat associated with 25 gypsum sinkholes;
- Conversion of non-productive farmlands to seasonal wetlands / moist soil units;
- Construction and upgrade of all-weather road for wildlife tour route.

Based on a review and evaluation of the information contained in the CCP and EA, I have determined that the approval of the individual or cumulative approaches reflected in the Proposed Alternative and CCP Goals, Objectives and Strategies, is not deemed to constitute a major Federal action which would significantly affect the quality of the human environment within the meaning of Section 102(2) (c) of the National Environmental Policy Act (NEPA). Therefore, an Environmental Impact Statement is not required. However, it is the intent of the

Service to revisit questions of potential significant environmental consequences in accordance with NEPA upon consideration of the implementation of site specific proposals called for and discussed in the final plan document.

_____ _____
Regional Director, Region 2   Date
U.S. Fish and Wildlife Service

eamfonsi.

Environmental Assessment

EA 1.0   Background

The Bitter Lake National Wildlife Refuge (NWR) consists of 24,536 acres in three units located along the Pecos River, northwest of Roswell, Chaves County, New Mexico. The North Tract occupies approximately 12,160 acres and encompasses the 9,620 acre, Salt Creek Wilderness. The Middle Tract is comprised of approximately 11,000 acres and contains the refuge headquarters, Bitter Lake, several sinkholes and natural wetlands, desert uplands, riparian areas, agricultural croplands and impoundments. The South Tract consists of approximately 1,000 of primarily agricultural crop land and is closed to all public access.

Bitter Lake NWR was established on October 8, 1937 by Executive Order 7724 "as a refuge and breeding ground for migratory birds and other wildlife." Additional laws direct station activities. These include the Migratory Bird Conservation Act (16 U.S.C. 715d), which identifies the refuge "for use as an inviolate sanctuary, or for any other management purpose, for migratory birds." The Refuge Recreation Act (16 U.S.C. 460-1) identifies the refuge as being "suitable for incidental fish and wildlife-oriented recreational development, the protection of natural resources, and the conservation of endangered species or threatened species." The Wilderness Act of 1964 (P.L. 88-577) directs the Service to "maintain wilderness as a naturally functioning ecosystem" on portions of the refuge.

While originally established to save wetlands vital to the perpetuation of migratory birds, the isolated gypsum springs, seeps, and associated wetlands protected by the refuge have been recognized as providing the last known habitats in the world for several unique species. Bitter Lake NWR provides habitat for at least 351 bird species, 57 mammal species, 51 reptile and amphibian species, and 24 fish species. Management emphasis on the refuge is placed on the protection and enhancement of habitat for endangered species and federal candidate species, maintenance and improvement of wintering crane and waterfowl habitat, and monitoring and maintenance of natural ecosystem values. Habitat management to maintain populations of important neotropical migrants, shorebirds, and resident species associated with the lower Pecos ecosystem are also major objectives. Large numbers of migratory birds utilize the refuge, supported by refuge wetlands on the Middle Tract, and irrigated crop land on the South Tract.

The refuge will be faced with a number of challenges and opportunities throughout the next 10 to 20 years including but not limited to the following:

- Maintenance and restoration of refuge facilities
- Maintenance of roads
- Production and efficient distribution of visitor information brochures
- Improving community outreach
- Oil and gas exploration and development issues
- Grazing pressures and cattle trespass

- Implementation of appropriate wilderness management for the Salt Creek Wilderness
- Non-native species control and removal
- Increasing and utilizing moist soils for waterfowl food production
- Revegetation of native species
- Increased interpretive information on the auto loop tour
- Land acquisition to improve management efforts and reduce encroachment by development
- Pecos River channel restoration

To address these issues, the Service has released a final Comprehensive Conservation Plan (CCP) for the Bitter Lake NWR. This final Environmental Assessment (EA) serves as a companion document. Both of these documents were published in draft form July 1, 1998, and submitted to the public for review and comment prior to the issuance of a final CCP.[1] Based upon input received during the comment period, the Service has made adjustments to its proposed alternative.

EA 2.0   Purpose and Need for the Proposed Action

The Service's Refuge Manual states that the purpose of comprehensive planning is to "provide long range guidance for the management of national wildlife refuges." [4 RM 1.1, Planning] Refuge comprehensive plans contain the set of issue-based management goals, objectives, strategies, and actions proposed for the short and long term. These constitute a proposed "management program" that is designed to address refuge issues (problems and opportunities) that will lead to the achievement of the refuge purposes, and ultimately, the mission of the National Wildlife Refuge System. Planning facilitates the kind of coordination that is necessary to enhance the efficiency of implementing management actions designed to benefit the Bitter Lake NWR and the surrounding area of ecological concern.

EA 3.0   Description of the Proposed Action & Alternatives

EA 3.1   Alternative A : (Proposed Action)

The proposed action is to adopt and implement the actions making up the Bitter Lake CCP. The objectives and strategies detailed in the plan will provide for short and long term conservation and enhancement of refuge resources and values in the planning area. The management actions within the proposed alternative reflect a need to continue the major strategies of restoring more than 1000 acres of upland habitat including grasslands, protecting and restoring wetland and riparian values, protecting wilderness values, protecting migratory bird resources. While the

---

[1] Federal Register, Vol 63, No. 126, p 35939, Notice of Intent to Issue 2 Draft Comprehensive Conservation Plans and Associated Environmental Assessments for 2 National Wildlife Refuges in the Southwest Region. This notice pertained to the release of the San Andres NWR and Bitter Lake NWR CCP/ EA draft documents.

proposed alternative calls for providing expanded wildlife observation and interpretive opportunities, there would be no expansion of hunting or fishing opportunities beyond the scope of the current program. Notable proposals in the program include:[2]

- Restoration of 250 acres of Research Natural Areas and 1000 acres in other areas by removal and control of non-native salt-cedar

- Restoration of over story vegetation near headquarters (10 acres) and providing appropriate irrigation

- Restore 140 acres of abandoned agricultural fields as grassland

- Promote education in area schools and organizations on the value of the short-grass prairie ecosystem

- Acquire appropriate land parcels as they become available on a willing seller basis

- Restoration of 100 acres of habitat associated with 25 gypsum sinkholes

- Conversion of non productive farmlands to seasonal wetlands / moist soil units

- Construction and upgrade of an all-weather road for wildlife tour route.

These actions among others would assist in the achievement of the following larger goals:

A. Restore, Enhance and Protect Biological Diversity, Land, Wildlife and Habitat

GOAL: To restore, enhance and protect the natural diversity on the Bitter Lake NWR including threatened and endangered species by: (1) appropriate management of habitat and wildlife resources on refuge lands; and (2) strengthening existing, and establishing new cooperative efforts with public and private stakeholders.

---

[2]The complete set of goals, objectives and strategies included in the proposed alternative can be referred to in Section 5.0 Bitter Lake NWR Management Program, (pg. 43 through 57), Bitter Lake NWR Final Comprehensive Conservation Plan, which accompanies this document.

B. Restore Hydrology and Improve Water Quality

GOAL: To restore and maintain a hydrological system that mimics the natural processes along the Pecos River drainage by: (1) restoration of the channel, as well as restoration of threatened, endangered and special concern species; and (2) control of exotic species and manage trust responsibilities for maintenance of plant and animal communities and to satisfy traditional recreational demands.

C. Provide Compatible Public Uses, Recreation, and Wildlife Interpretation & Educational.

GOAL: To offer compatible wildlife-dependent public access and recreational opportunities to include compatible forms of hunting, wildlife observation and photography, and continue wildlife interpretation and educational efforts.

D. Protect Cultural Resources

GOAL: To protect, and maintain cultural resources on the Bitter Lake NWR for the benefit of present and future generations.

E. Strengthen and Maintain Effective Relationships with Other Governmental Agencies and Groups to Enhance Coordination.

GOALS: To strengthen interagency and jurisdictional relationships in order to coordinate efforts with respect to refuge and surrounding area issues, resulting in decisions benefitting fish and wildlife resources, while at the same time avoiding duplication of effort.

F. Improve Refuge Staffing and Funding

GOAL: To effect improvements to staffing and funding that will result in long-term enhancement of habitat and wildlife resources in the area of ecological concern, and allow the achievement of goals of this plan and the goals of the National Wildlife Refuge System.

EA 3.2   Alternative B: (No Action Alternative)

This alternative would focus on the continuation of management of existing conditions and facilities and would not involve extensive riparian restoration efforts, development of moist soil units from unproductive farm land, extensive upland habitat restoration, and improvements to interpretive facilities, roads and administrative facilities. There would be no further land acquisition efforts to tie together existing refuge units.

EA 3.3   Alternative C

This alternative would incorporate the changes to the habitat and wildlife management component of the program called for in the proposed alternative. However, in addition to an expansion of wildlife observation and interpretive opportunities, this alternative would also expand compatible fishing and hunting opportunities beyond the existing program.

EA 4.0   Affected Environment

A description of the affected environment can be found in *Section 3.0* of the Final Comprehensive Conservation Plan for Bitter Lake NWR Comprehensive Conservation Plan.

EA 5.0   Environmental Consequences

The following brief discussions and informal analyses pertain to key environmental issues and their relationship with each of the Alternatives considered in this document.

EA 5.1   Alternative A (Proposed Action)

EA 5.1.1   Biological Resources

This alternative involves the expansion of existing efforts to restore upland habitat including extensive removal of non-native vegetation, restoring grasslands, protecting and extensively restoring wetland and riparian values, protecting wilderness values, and protecting migratory bird resources. The alternative also involves the expansion of compatible wildlife observation, photography and educational opportunities.

Salt Cedar Removal. Efforts involving the removal of non-native salt cedar in riparian areas would only minimally effect avian uses. Removal of salt cedar will have positive consequences for natural germination of native willows and cottonwood. Removal of salt cedar would also eliminate unwanted fuel, thus preventing fire. Use of mechanical means and/or herbicides would be selective and impacts would be temporary.

Restoration of Grasslands. No negative impacts would occur as a result of efforts to convert 140 acres of abandoned agricultural fields to native grassland.

Restoration of Wetlands. The creation of moist soil habitat from non-productive farm fields would increase the wildlife use and improve migratory bird diversity.

Construction and Upgrade of Roads. This project would have short term and very temporary minimal impacts. No roads would be widened to any great extent. Upgrade of the road would minimize soil erosion and eliminate the need for frequent maintenance. Conversion to an all-weather road would eliminate profusion of particulate matter into the air from vehicle use.

Restoration to habitat from gypsum sinkholes. This effort would create 100 new acres of habitat and would result in positive impacts for refuge wildlife.

Fire Management. Nothing proposed in this alternative pertaining to fire management would permanently impact refuge biological resources. Prescribed burning would be designed to enhance habitat while eliminating unwanted fuel, thus preventing unwanted wild fires. Suppression and pre-suppression strategies would be conducted in accordance with Service policy and designed to minimally affect habitat resources (i.e. firebreaks). Pre-suppression strategies would be designed to maximize suppression capabilities in the event of a fire outbreak. Impacts would be moderate and temporary and would be designed to enhance the natural biological diversity of the landscape.

Enhancement of Opportunities for Wildlife Observation & Photography. These proposed enhancements will have little or no effect on biological resources except to improve the publics access to and understanding of them. Construction of kiosks, signs and interpretive panels would be of limited scope and not result in any negative impacts to the refuge biological resources.

Other management actions. Nothing noted in the management program for the refuge would negatively affect refuge wildlife, fish, plant, and habitat resources.

EA 5.1.2   Air Quality

Expanded uses of fire as a management tool on the refuge would cause slight and temporary impacts to refuge's air quality if Alternative A is adopted. Prescribed fires would be managed and monitored in accordance with Service policy. Lack of a good pre-suppression and suppression capability would probably result in larger and more intense fires. Road upgrades might cause a very slight but temporary profusion of particulate matter into the air.

EA 5.1.3   Water Quality

Alternative A provides for the general improvement of the refuge's wetland and riparian areas to include better monitoring of water quality standards. Nothing in the alternative is anticipated to negatively impact water quality on Service lands.

EA 5.1.4   Wetland Preservation and Enhancement

Alternative A provides for the continuation of and enhancement to activities that improve the Service's wetland and riparian resources. Nothing in the alternative is anticipated to negatively impact wetland resources.

EA 5.1.5   Cultural Resources

The cultural resource component of the Bitter Lake NWR lands is significant and any site specific proposals that might alter or effect the landscape will have to be considered in the context of potential effects to cultural and archeological resources. However, nothing in the proposed alternative is anticipated to negatively effect the refuge's cultural, historical, and archeological resources. Goal 4 of the proposed action calls for the specific protection of all refuge cultural resources.

EA 5.1.   Socioeconomics

Nothing in the proposed alternative is anticipated to have negative effects to the economic or social context of the refuge lands. It is expected that the alternative's proposal for opening selected tracts for wildlife-dependent public recreation and access will provide an economic benefit to the overall economic region. For ecotourism alone, visitors can spend between $21 and $145 dollars during a visit to the local community. All refuges, like other federal lands, are important economic assets to both the national economy and the economies of the communities in which they are located.[3] A combination of local visitors and those from farther away provide a source of revenue, enhancing the multiplier effect created by the constant flow of money.

EA 5.2   Alternative B (No Action)

EA 5.2.1   Biological Resources

Alternative B offers a strong level of protection for the biological resources on the refuge although without a set of updated goals and strategies. By adopting the "no action" alternative, the Refuge would anticipate no negative impacts to the overall landscape. Unlike the proposed alternative, efforts to revegetate lands and restore wetlands would be limited in scope. While continuing existing strategies and approaches would have no negative affects on biological resources, a lack of a strategic context of publicly accepted goals and strategies would make it more difficult for land managers to implement resource priorities. Indirectly, this could slow progress towards improving habitat and wildlife conditions refuge wide.

EA 5.2.2   Air Quality

There are no negative impacts anticipated to air quality by adoption of Alternative B.

EA 5.2.3   Water Quality

No negative effects are anticipated should Alternative B be adopted. The refuge would continue to monitor, to the degree possible, water quality in cooperation with the State. Without a strategic context, it is difficult to determine the priority of this issue.

EA 5.2.4   Wetland Preservation and Enhancement

Under Alternative B the refuge would continue efforts on a more limited basis to rehabilitate existing wetlands. Nothing proposed in

---

[3] Kerlinger, Paul Phd, Ted Eubanks, R.H. Payne, 1994, The Economic Impact of Birding Ecotourism on communities Surrounding Eight National Wildlife Refuges, New Jersey Audubon Society.

this alternative is anticipated to have negative effects on the human environment.

EA 5.2.5 Compatibility and Service Policy on Recreational Uses

Under this alternative, the Service would not establish new recreational uses for the refuge other than those currently in place. Enhancements to opportunities for wildlife observation and photography would not affect current compatibility determinations.

EA 5.2.6 Cultural Resources

Under this alternative, there would be no effects from the management of the refuge's cultural resources. As new lands are acquired, cultural resource assessments would have to be conducted in accordance with Service policy and in coordination with the State Historic Preservation Officer.

EA 5.2.7 Socioeconomics

The adoption of Alternative B would not result in the employment of strategies that would negatively affect the human environment including the economy of the Roswell area.

EA 5.3 Alternative C

EA 5.3.1 Biological Resources

Like Alternative A (Proposed), this alternative involves the expansion of existing efforts to restore upland habitat including extensive removal of non-native vegetation, restoring grasslands, protecting and extensively restoring wetland and riparian values, protecting wilderness values, and protecting migratory bird resources. In addition to the expansion of compatible wildlife observation, photography and educational opportunities, hunting and fishing opportunities would be expanded if determined compatible.

The expansion of compatible fishing and hunting opportunities differentiates this alternative from Alternative A. The expansion of these activities, even if determined compatible, would have certain negative impacts (although minor) on habitat, plants and wildlife species depending locations chosen, the level of control imposed on the hunt, and the duration of the hunts. Expansion of fishing opportunities could affect endangered fish recovery efforts and any such efforts would necessitate analysis with respect to the requirements of Section 7 of the Endangered Species Act. Previous compatibility determinations on hunting and fishing on the refuge would need to be revisited. Compatibility determinations for the expansion of any such proposed uses beyond the current program would have to be undertaken prior to implementation. Coordination with the New Mexico Department of Game and Fish would need to take place.

EA 5.3.2   Air Quality

As in the case of the proposed alternative, expanded uses of fire as a management tool on the refuge would cause slight and temporary impacts to refuge's air quality if Alternative C is adopted. Prescribed fires would be managed and monitored in accordance with Service policy. Lack of a good pre-suppression and suppression capability would probably result in larger and more intense fires. Road upgrades might cause a very slight but temporary profusion of particulate matter into the air. There would be no effect to air quality as a result of the adoption of Alternative C.

EA 5.3.3   Water Quality

Like Proposed Alternative A, Alternative C provides for the general improvement of the refuge's wetland and riparian areas to include better monitoring of water quality standards. Nothing in the alternative is anticipated to negatively impact water quality on Service lands.

EA 5.3.4   Wetland Preservation and Enhancement

Like Alternative A, Alternative C provides for the continuation of and enhancement to activities that improve the Service's wetland and riparian resources. Nothing in the alternative is anticipated to negatively impact wetland resources. The alternative may positively affect wetland and riparian resources.

EA 5.3.5 Compatibility and Service Policy on Recreational Uses

This alternative calls for the possible expansion of all forms of priority wildlife-dependent forms of recreation if determined compatible. Compatibility determinations for the expansion of any such proposed uses beyond the current program would have to be undertaken prior to implementation. Coordination with the New Mexico Department of Game and Fish would need to take place.

EA 5.3.6 Cultural Resources

The cultural resource component of the Bitter Lake NWR lands is significant and any site specific proposals that might alter or effect the landscape will have to be considered in the context of potential effects to cultural and archeological resources. However, nothing in the proposed alternative is anticipated to negatively effect the refuge's cultural, historical, and archeological resources provided all actions are in compliance with the Archeological Resources Protection Act, the National Historic Preservation Act, and other cultural resource laws.

EA 5.3.7 Socioeconomics

Adoption of this alternative would have no negative impacts on the local economies. Eco-tourism would improve with expanded opportunities for wildlife observation, photography and interpretation. Additional hunting and fishing opportunities would also positively affect refuge visitation.

EA 6.0 Cumulative Impacts, Mitigation and Consultation and Coordination

EA 6.1 Cumulative Impacts

Cumulative impacts include impacts on the environment which result from incremental effects of the proposed action when added to other past, present, and reasonably foreseeable future actions. Cumulative impacts can result from individually minor, but collectively significant actions taking place over a period of time. Implementing Alternative A would reduce any potential for cumulative impacts because of the strategic approach to managing refuge programs including wildlife-dependent public uses, and the consideration of resource conflicts and opportunities within a broad management framework. This would be a change from the issue-by-issue, problem-by-problem fragmented approach inherent in the No Action alternative.

Where site development activities are to be proposed during the next 5 to 10 years, each activity would be given any additional appropriate NEPA consideration. At that time, any required mitigation activities if any are necessary, would be designed into the specific project to reduce the level of impacts to the human environment and to protect fish and wildlife and their habitats.

EA 6.2   Mitigation Measures

Mitigation measures are necessary when effects are anticipated to be at the threshold of significance. Nothing proposed in Alternative A would produce environmental impacts that are near any level of significance so as to warrant mitigation measures. However, the activities listed below help reduce the risks that any negative effect will occur. Long-term monitoring will help in determining actual effects and how the Service should respond.

- The refuge would closely regulate any proposed activities to lessen any potential impacts such as restricting use to seasons and locations when known breeding and nesting activities are at a minimum.

- The refuge would prohibit any activities in areas where endangered species would be negatively affected.

EA 6.3   Consultation and Coordination

In an ongoing effort to involve the local community and officials in the CCP process, the Service and Research Management Consultants Inc. (RMCI) prepared and distributed a fact sheet in August 1997. The fact sheet describes the CCP process and defined the comment period. The fact sheet was mailed in early August 1997 and the 45-day comment period started August 25, 1997 and ended October 8, 1997. An information repository has also been established and is maintained with information relevant to the refuge for public review. The repository is located at the Roswell Public Library in Alamagordo, New Mexico. RMCI continues to update the mailing list based on response from interested parties. Public meetings may be provided if necessary, based on public response to the CCP process. A draft CCP and Environmental Assessment (EA) were released July 1, 1998. The Service published a formal notice in the Federal Register requesting comments and advice from the public.[4] Comments were received,

---

[4] Federal Register, Vol 63, No. 126, p 35939, Notice of Intent to Issue 2 Draft Comprehensive Conservation Plans and Associated Environmental Assessments for 2 National Wildlife Refuges in the Southwest Region. This notice pertained to the release of the San Andres NWR and Bitter Lake NWR CCP/ EA draft documents.

considered, and to the degree possible, they have been incorporated into this document.

EA 7.0   EA Document Preparation

Thomas P. Baca, M.P.A., Senior Natural Resource Planner, Division of Refuges and Realty, Branch of Biological Support and Planning, U.S. Fish and Wildlife Service, Southwest Region, Albuquerque, NM.

www.ingramcontent.com/pod-product-compliance
Lightning Source LLC
Chambersburg PA
CBHW081213280526
45787CB00006B/2396